BETHLEHEM STEEL

RUSTING RELIC

STEVEN M. LANDIS AND JOHN K. LANDIS

AMERICA
THROUGH
TIME

America Through Time
An imprint of Sutton Publishing Inc
www.through-time.com

First published 2023
Reprinted 2024, 2025

ISBN 978-1-63499-493-4

Typeset in Sabon 10pt on 12pt
Printed and bound in England

PREFACE

Bethlehem Steel was once number eight on the annual Fortune 500 listing of America's largest and most financially successful corporations, and the fluctuations of its publicly traded stock prices on the New York Stock Exchange were a bellwether of the nation's economy. This industrial giant no longer exists, but at the flagship site of Bethlehem, Pennsylvania, we are fortunate to have five blast furnaces and a number of buildings extant on a fraction of the original property. They are vestiges of the past, left by this once-great icon of American industry.

As a tour guide for Historic Bethlehem Museums and Sites, I use these skeletal sentinels as the backdrop for my version of "The Rise and Fall of Bethlehem Steel," the name of the tour that I have presented hundreds of times to visitors from all over the world.

Steven M. Landis, the photographer and caption writer of the images contained in this book, had rare sanctioned access to the plant facilities during 2006, permitting extraordinary photographs, many of which will never be achievable again because the location is closed to the public or simply does not exist anymore.

Accompanying the photography is an abridged overview of making things out of metal on this historically significant ground, including who began it all, how iron and steel were made, who worked at the plant, and what caused the ultimate demise of "The Steel." The narrative hardly purports to be a definitive company history, already written many times. It is instead an expansion of topics that I mention on my tours, including directing attention to surviving plant remnants still visible today.

The interlacing of the book's photos and the historical overview is intended to provide an enhanced appreciation of the aesthetic beauty of industrial artifacts, with recognition of the substantial and enduring mark in history made by Bethlehem Steel.

John K. Landis
Bethlehem, Pennsylvania
March 2023

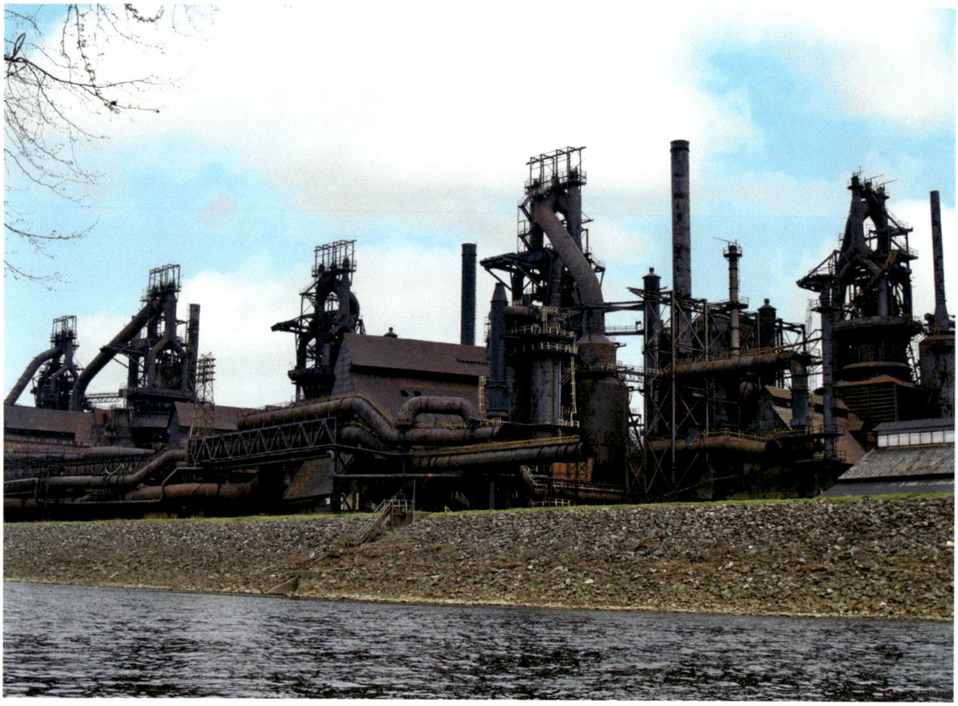

The five remaining blast furnaces from across the Lehigh River in 2008. *From right to left*: Blast Furnaces A, B, C, D, and E.

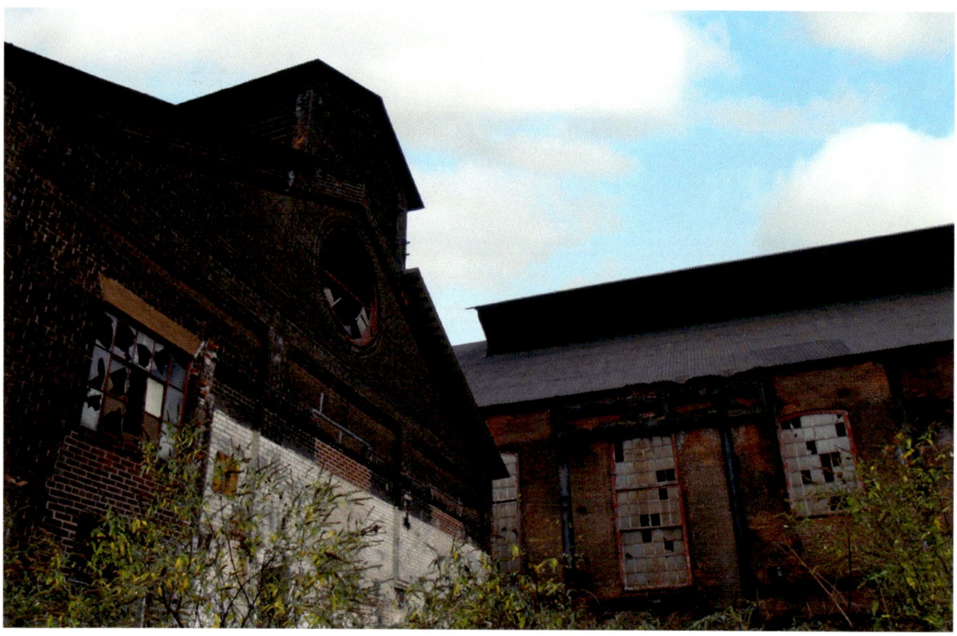

Abandoned buildings at the former flagship Bethlehem Steel plant.

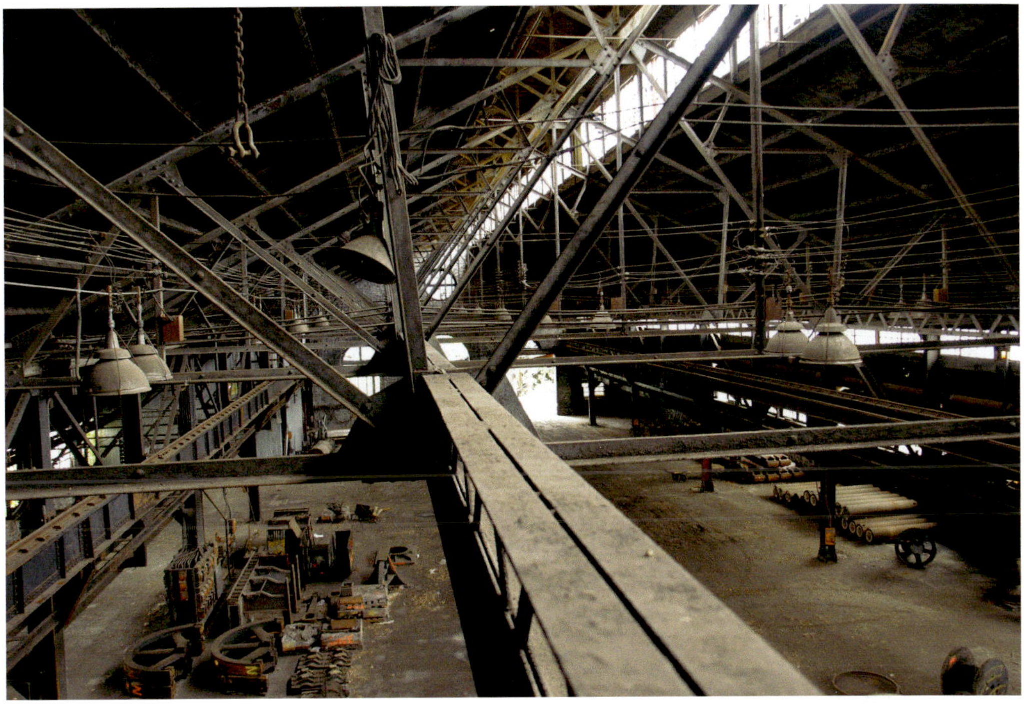

Above: View from the rafters in the Turn & Grind Shop.

Right: A group of visitors on top of the Hoover-Mason Trestle for one of John K. Landis's tours in 2023. He appears in the white hard hat.

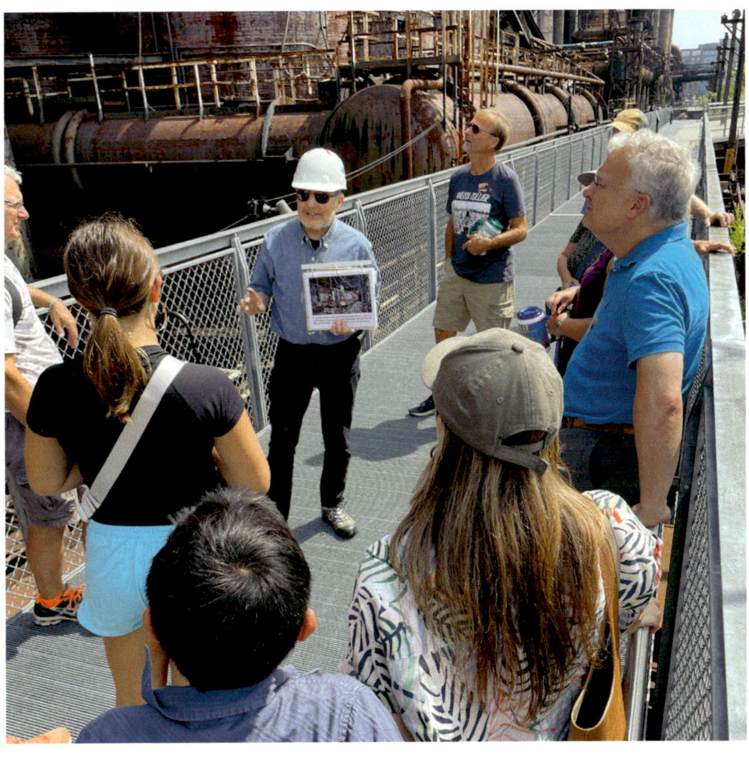

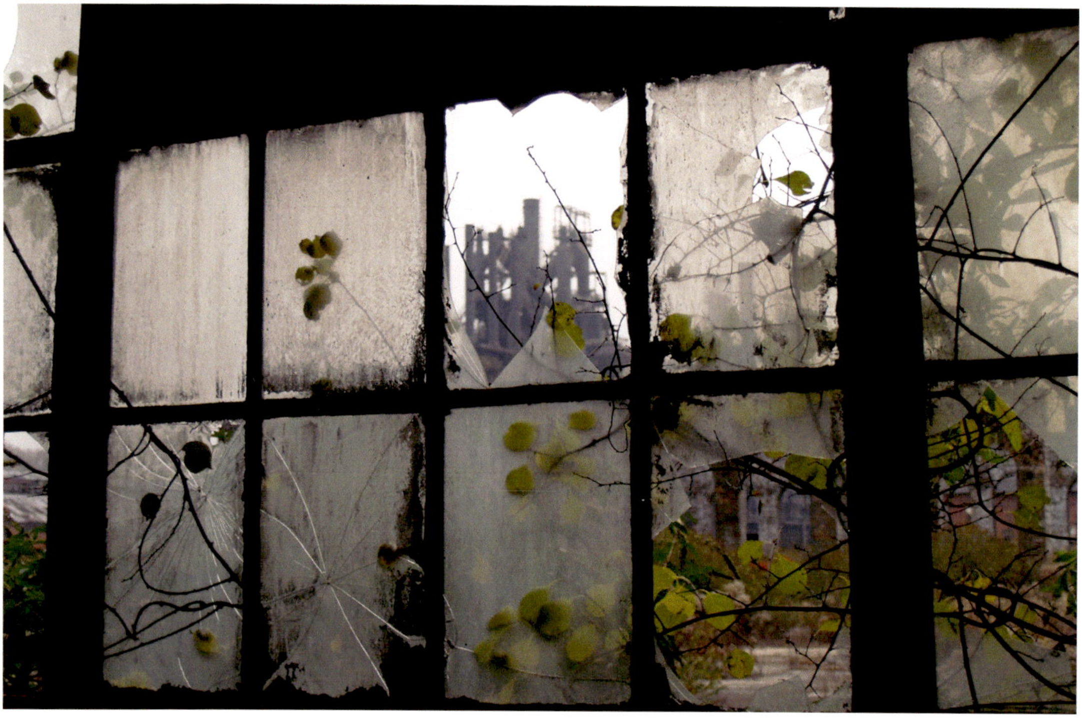

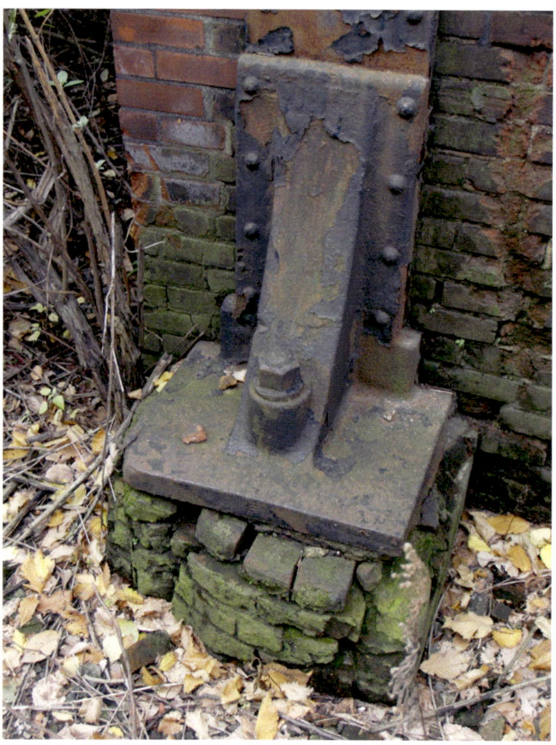

Above: A blast furnace through one of the Bethlehem Steel plant's many broken windows.

Left: Vintage wall reinforcement.

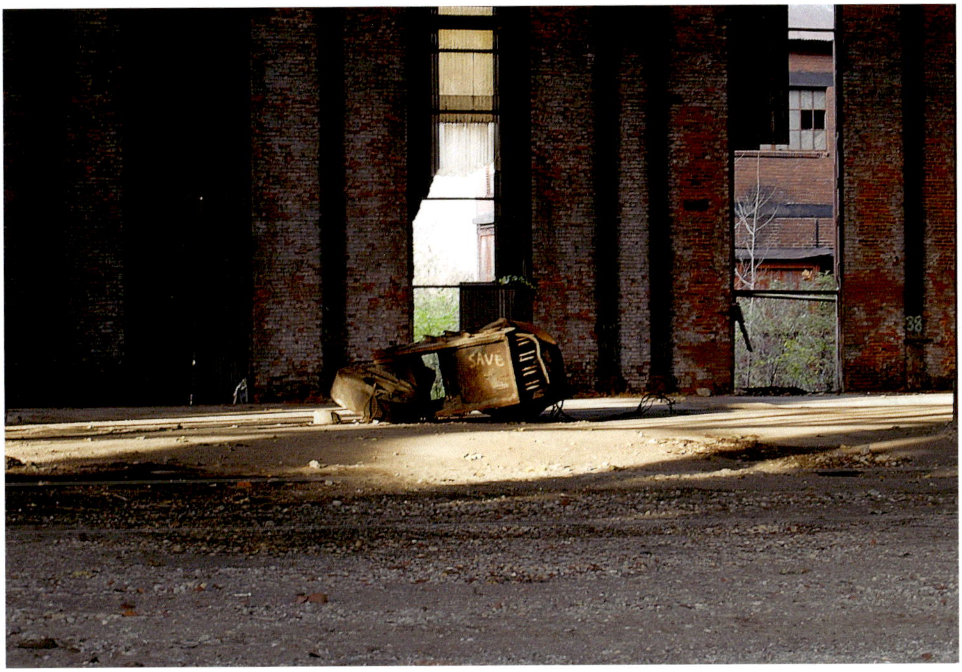

An industrial remnant beckons to be saved.

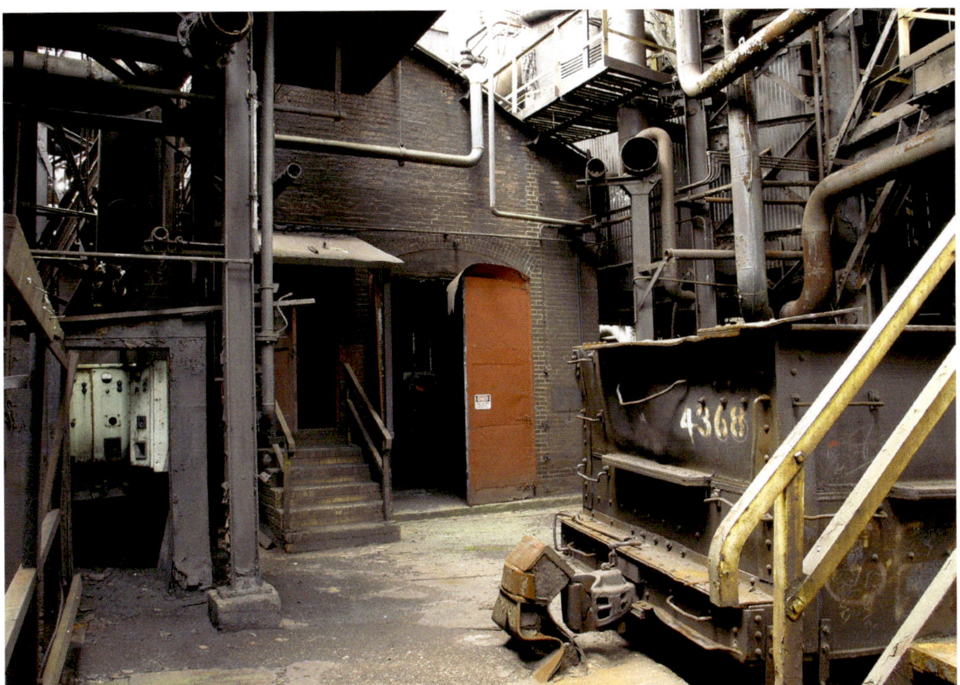

A railroad car waits in between the blast furnaces along "blast furnace row."

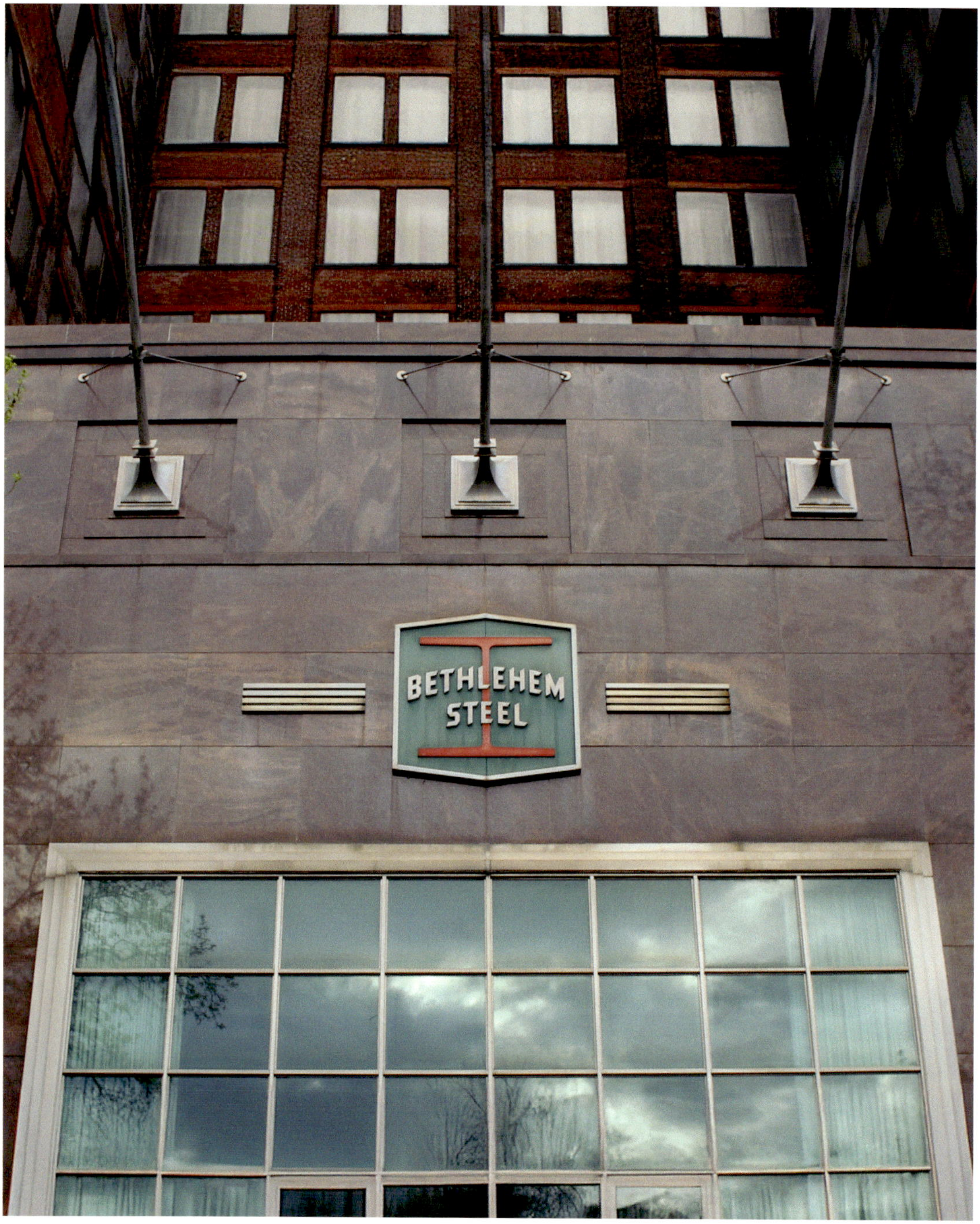

The abandoned General Office still retains its vintage Bethlehem Steel signage. Photograph taken in 2023.

ACKNOWLEDGMENTS

With special thanks to John K. Landis, my dad and professor emeritus of Kutztown University, Pennsylvania State System of Higher Education, who helped inspire me to finally find a way to publish my Bethlehem Steel photographs and whose main text of this book gives them their needed context.

Thank you to Alison Landis Stone, my sister and professional editor, for her editing of the manuscript and for gifting me Alex Gulino's *Empire State of Decay: Discarded New York*.

Thank you to Alex Gulino—your gorgeous America Through Time photography books influenced me to contact Fonthill Media.

Thank you to Kraig L. Marini Baker, professor at the University of Washington and partner at the Davis, Wright, Tremaine LLC Law Firm, for his legal review of the manuscript.

Thank you to Kathy M. Landis, my mom, for reviewing the text and for offering thought-provoking and spiritual guidance.

Thank you to Barbara Schulman, my dad's wife, for reviewing the text for general understanding.

Thank you to Alan Sutton, Kena Longabaugh, Jasper Hadman, Jamie Hardwick, and Fonthill Media for this opportunity and for their patience during multiple delays as I tried to get everything in this book "just right."

Thank you to David Rehrig for the use of your photograph on page 12.

Additional thanks to my uncle James Marshall, my aunt Anne Homan, and my cousin Andy Homan for the inspiration I obtained from your books.

I am honored by all the love and support that Stephania Jhaya, my girlfriend, has given to me and to the promotion of this book. ¡Gracias y te amo mucho!

Steven M. Landis

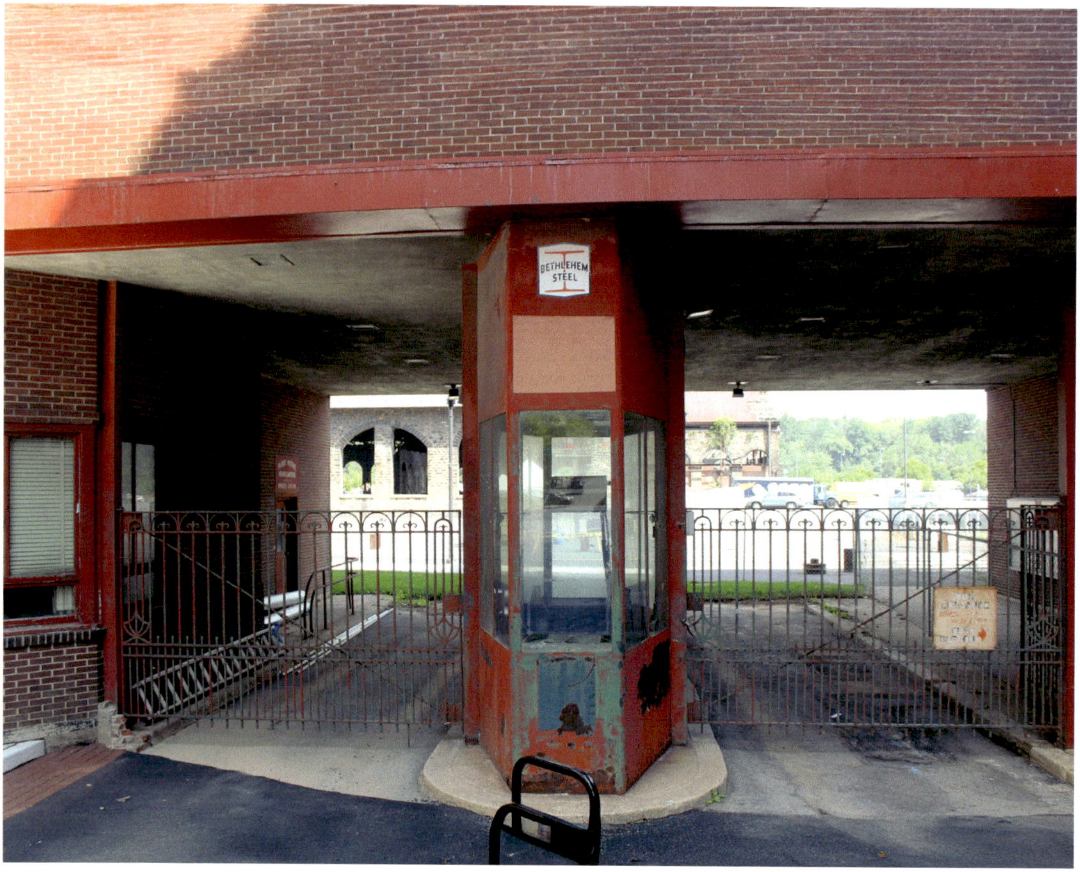

A preserved entrance gate to the Bethlehem Steel plant. Immediately below the Bethlehem Steel logo, the heavily faded text reads “The Employees of the Bethlehem Plant Welcome You!” Photograph taken in 2023.

CONTENTS

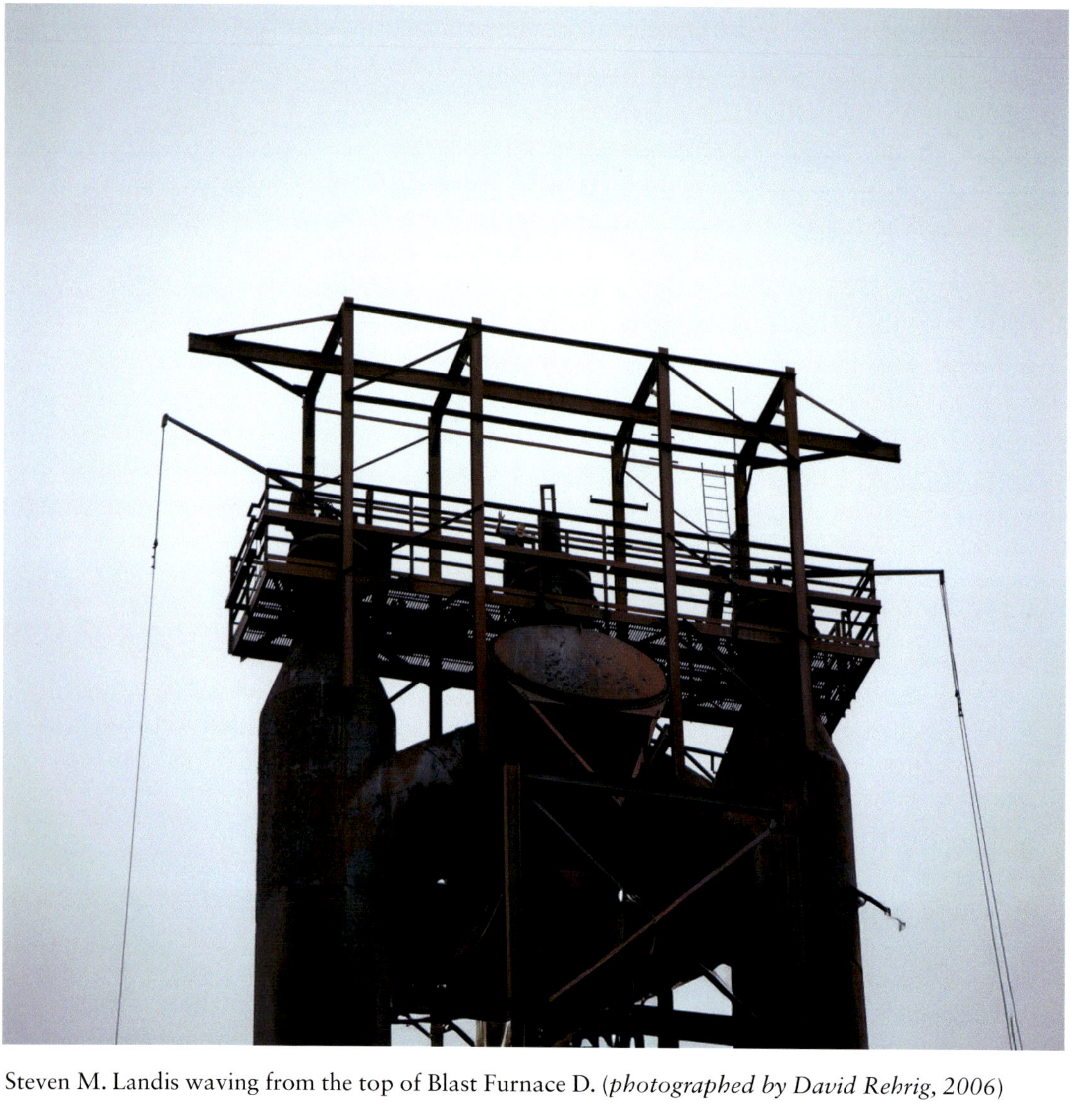

Steven M. Landis waving from the top of Blast Furnace D. (*photographed by David Rehrig, 2006*)

INTRODUCTION

When describing where I live to those outside of Pennsylvania, I have frequently referenced the famous 1982 Billy Joel song, "Allentown." However, the inspiration of his song was actually Bethlehem Steel, which was not based in Allentown. Billy Joel had struggled to create rhyming lyrics with "Bethlehem," and that name further carried religious connotations that could distract from the blue-collar anthem. So, he instead chose to use "Allentown"—the immediate neighboring city that is closely economically tied with the city of Bethlehem, Pennsylvania—as the name of his song. As the song soared in popularity, it helped put both Bethlehem and Allentown "on the map" for a large audience.

Twice in 2006, I joined a small group that obtained authorization to visit the former Bethlehem Steel plant in Bethlehem, Pennsylvania. These were incredible experiences for me. Growing up in the 1980s and 1990s, I had seen, smelled, heard, and felt Bethlehem Steel when it was still operational. It teemed with life from thousands of workers operating around the clock. The plant itself also appeared to be its own living thing as it inhaled vast loads of taconite, coke, and limestone; belched a pall of smoke and ash; poured out train carloads of glowing molten iron; and for nearly a century and a half made iron and steel for bridges, buildings, dams, railroad rail, ships, armor plating, armaments, and a huge variety of other products that created and protected the world we know.

Walking and climbing among the ruins of the shuttered plant, I could still feel the energy there. Some areas retained an appearance of the workers only being on a lunch break, ready to return to their jobs at any moment. Other areas of the plant were already showing heavy signs of dilapidation after being abandoned "only" a decade earlier (1995 was the last cast "hot end" operation for the Bethlehem plant). The entire site for me held an air of veiled sorrow, of missed opportunity, and of what-ifs. But, within this rusting relic of American industry, I also saw overwhelming beauty in the duality of decay and stubborn perseverance of some of the structures as they were slowly being reclaimed by nature. I felt awestruck by the memories and lessons the plant continues to evoke even in its derelict condition.

My dad began offering "Steel" tours for Historic Bethlehem Museums and Sites in 2019 after retiring from a nearly forty-year career of university teaching and working in the communication design industry. He asked me for my photographs of the Bethlehem Steel plant as visuals for his tour groups that would never be authorized access to the abandoned buildings or blast furnaces, instead only walking around a fenced outer perimeter. (Considerable sections of the former plant are now altogether gone and have been replaced by a casino, a hotel, restaurants, shopping, and an entertainment complex.) Joining one of my dad's tours and enjoying "the show," as the large group clung to his every word and huddled tightly to see 8 × 10 prints of my photographs in a portfolio he held up, inspired me to create the book you are holding now. I hope you enjoy this armchair tour of the former flagship Bethlehem Steel plant in Bethlehem, Pennsylvania.

None of my photographs were taken with the use of a drone. Unless the photograph caption specifies otherwise, I took all photographs in 2006 on the site of the former Bethlehem Steel plant. I predominantly worked with an Olympus E-500 digital camera (all 2006 photographs), but also used a Canon Rebel T6 digital camera and an Apple iPhone 12 for more recent photographs.

Steven M. Landis
Allentown, Pennsylvania
March 2023

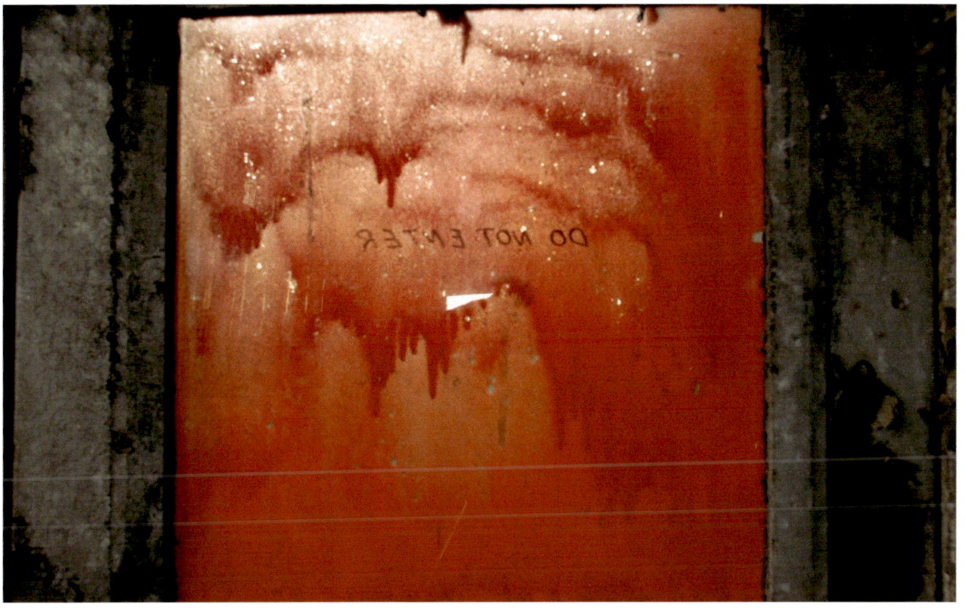

Photographed from inside, this door once warned workers to find another point of entry, but the doors to this armchair tour are now all wide open to you …

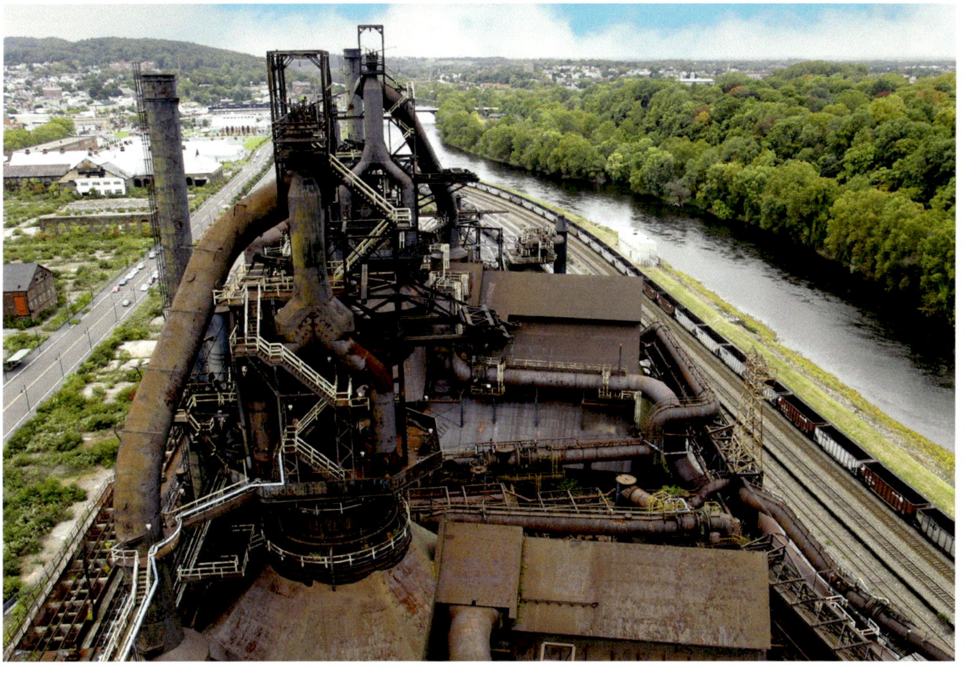

Looking upriver from the top of Blast Furnace D. Blast Furnace C fills much of the frame, followed by Blast Furnace B. An active multi-track railroad closely abuts the Lehigh River on the right. This photograph was taken roughly 100 feet higher than the cover photograph.

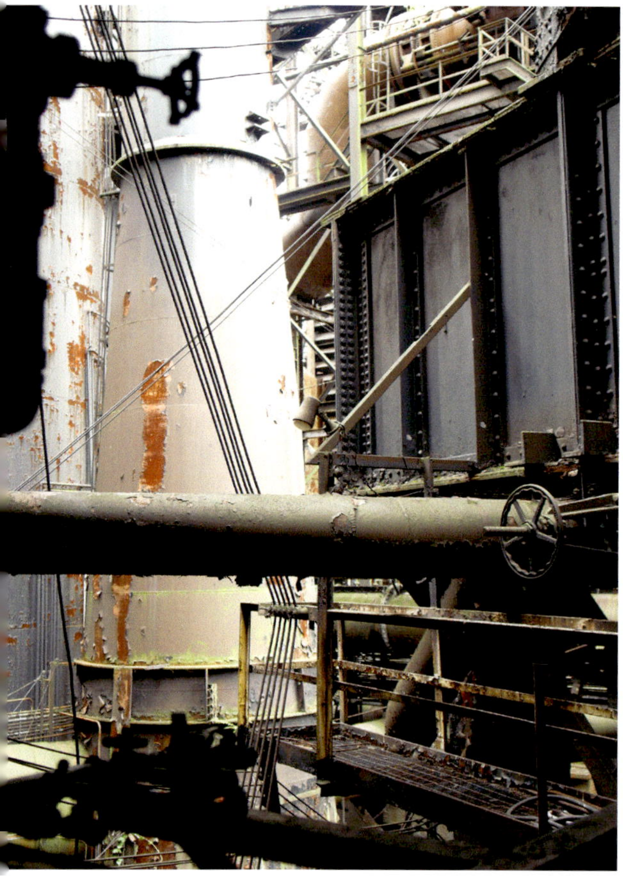

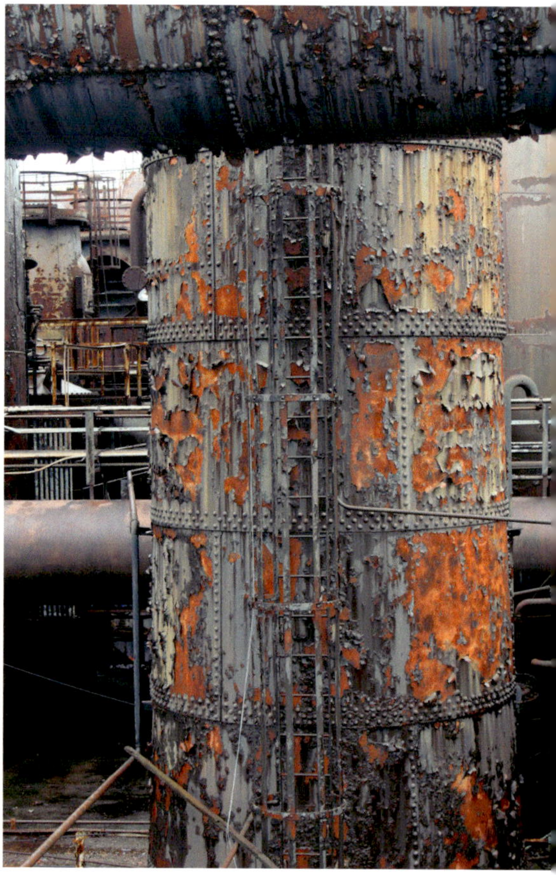

Above left: The variety of industrial colors, patinas, shapes, patterns, and textures on the grounds of the former Bethlehem Steel plant endlessly entertains the "urban exploration" photographer's eye.

Above right: Yet further demonstrating the incredible visual interest of the plant. Photograph taken in 2023.

1

THE MORAVIANS, A RIVER, AND A RAILROAD

What is today the city of Bethlehem traces its origins to the year 1741, well before the American Revolution. In that year the Moravians, a religious group from an area of today's Czech Republic, were deeded 500 acres of land where the Monocacy Creek empties into the Lehigh River. The Moravians were an ingenious people who floated logs down the river to their settlement and then hollowed them out to make pipes. By 1762, they had created what is considered the first water-pumping system in the colonies.

Metal also figured prominently in Moravian craft work. They used copper and zinc to make cooking utensils and iron to make horseshoes, hinges, and farm implements. It was the making of metal products of those many years ago that began a legacy that would define the very image of American heavy industry: steelmaking.

In 1852, a railroad was built following the river. Named the North Penn Railroad, it evolved into today's Norfolk Southern Railway, still very visible between the river and the remaining blast furnaces. To support iron and steel production on an industrial scale in Bethlehem, the railroad was necessary to bring in raw materials and take out heavy finished products.

It was on this ground along the Lehigh River that an industrial giant would develop: a prosperous American company known as "The Steel" that would make a product in great demand, worldwide, for nearly a century and a half.

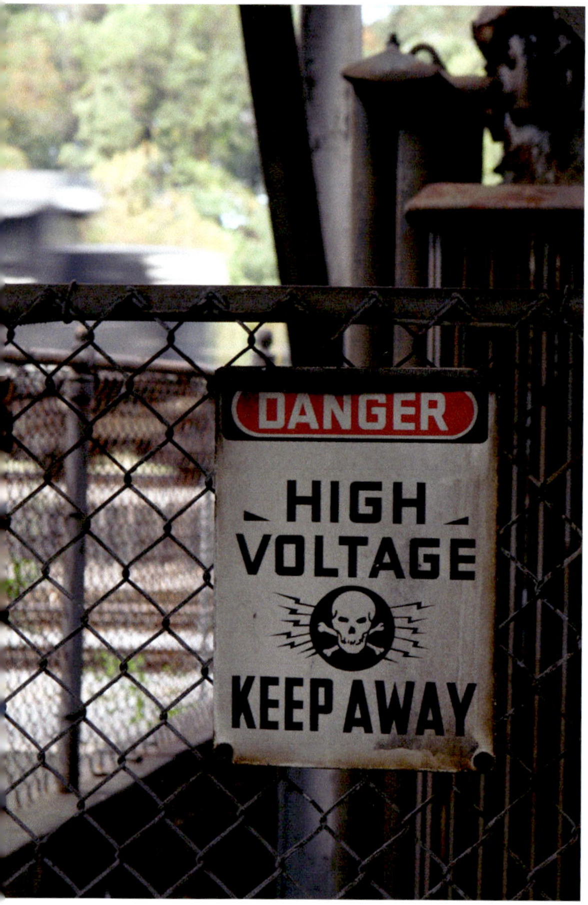

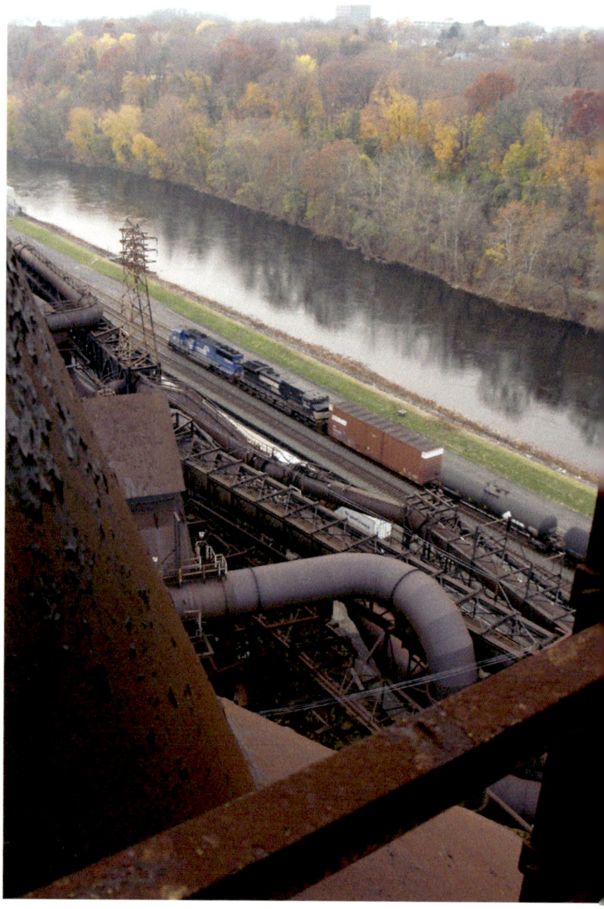

Above left: A menacing high-voltage warning sign demands attention as a diesel locomotive approaches behind the chain-link fence.

Above right: A train rumbles past the shuttered Bethlehem Steel plant, no longer commanding the frequent freight stops that it once did. The Lehigh River rolls lazily along in the opposite direction.

2

EARLY PERSONALITIES OF BETHLEHEM STEEL

Several early innovators and financial risktakers could be considered the first employees of Bethlehem Steel. Bethlehem Steel's origins trace back to 1857 with the founding of Saucona Iron Company. In the early 1860s, when the U.S. was in the Civil War, Robert Sayre (1824–1907) laid out the design and supervised construction of the renamed Bethlehem Iron Company. Sayre was vice president and chief engineer of the Lehigh Valley Railroad, an undertaking that was financed by Asa Packer (1805–1879), a politician and canal boat owner who perceived that it would be the railroads, not canals, that would foster America's golden age of industrial development. With an initial donation of 57 acres of land and $500,000, Packer is best remembered for founding Lehigh University as a technical trade school for engineers in 1865.

Various early creative efforts in metallurgical industrialization were pulled together by Charles M. Schwab (1862–1939), an aggressive investor who bought up stock of several smaller iron companies and consolidated them into what would become Bethlehem Steel. He had been a protégé of Andrew Carnegie and was the first president of United States Steel Corporation. He is a different Schwab from the investment firm founder Charles R. Schwab.

It took strong and bold personalities to build a new industry that would eventually reach far beyond the wooded banks of the Lehigh River. Early entrepreneurs in the industrial development of nineteenth-century America had an unstoppable will that would not be satisfied with anything short of realizing their daring dreams and visions.

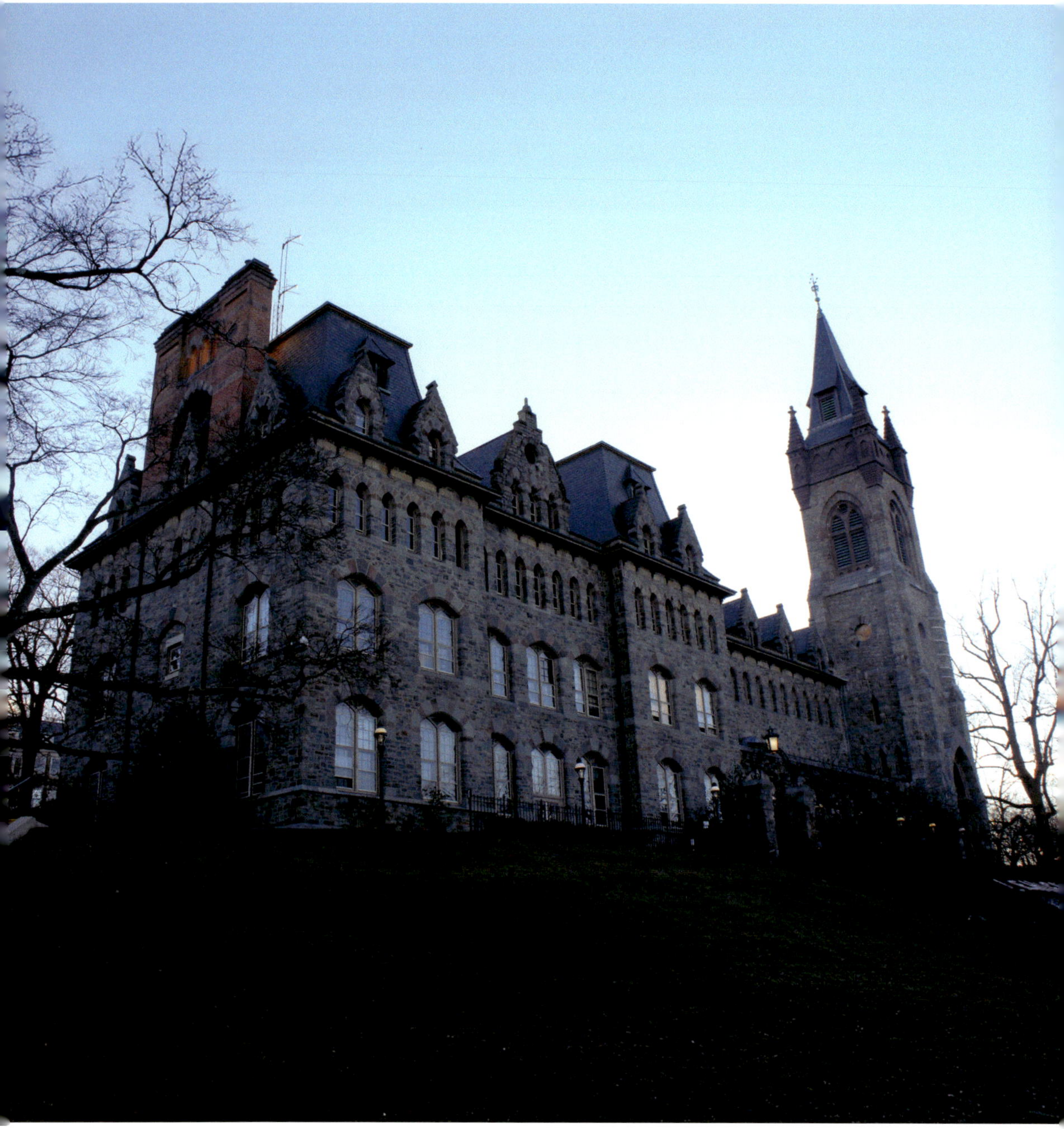

University Center (Packer Hall), Lehigh University, in 2021.

3

THE RAW MATERIALS OF STEELMAKING

Steelmaking began by producing molten iron, using three raw materials introduced into a blast furnace, the historical icon of a steel mill.

First was taconite, a low-grade iron ore, comprised of various elements, with iron being predominant. An ore is a rock from which a useful element can be economically obtained. Bethlehem Steel's major sources of taconite were three mines in eastern Pennsylvania, although some was sourced from open-pit and underground mining in Canada, Central and South America, and even Liberia, Africa. Taconite is broken up into pieces and mixed with clay and water and shaped into balls a little smaller than marbles. These pellets were easy to transport and consistent in shape for ease of smelting, heating to a high temperature beyond the melting point, in the blast furnace.

The second material was coke, the fuel source to smelt the taconite. Coke is coal heated to a very high temperature in the absence of oxygen, removing moisture and impurities and leaving almost pure carbon. It burns hotter and cleaner than coal. Bethlehem Steel mostly used bituminous, called soft coal, mined in West Virginia, but also in western Pennsylvania and Kentucky. It was "coked" in Hellertown, Pennsylvania, just a few miles from the steel mills. Historically, charcoal, wood heated to a high temperature with restricted air access (similar to coking), was the heat source for smelting iron ore.

The third ingredient was limestone, the fossilized skeletal remains of tiny sea creatures from the Ordovician Period in geological history, 500 million years ago, when a vast inland sea covered much of North America. Limestone acts as a flux to encourage the taconite and coke to merge and turn into liquid form. It also removes impurities from the mixture. Bethlehem Steel obtained limestone from its own quarries in South Central Pennsylvania.

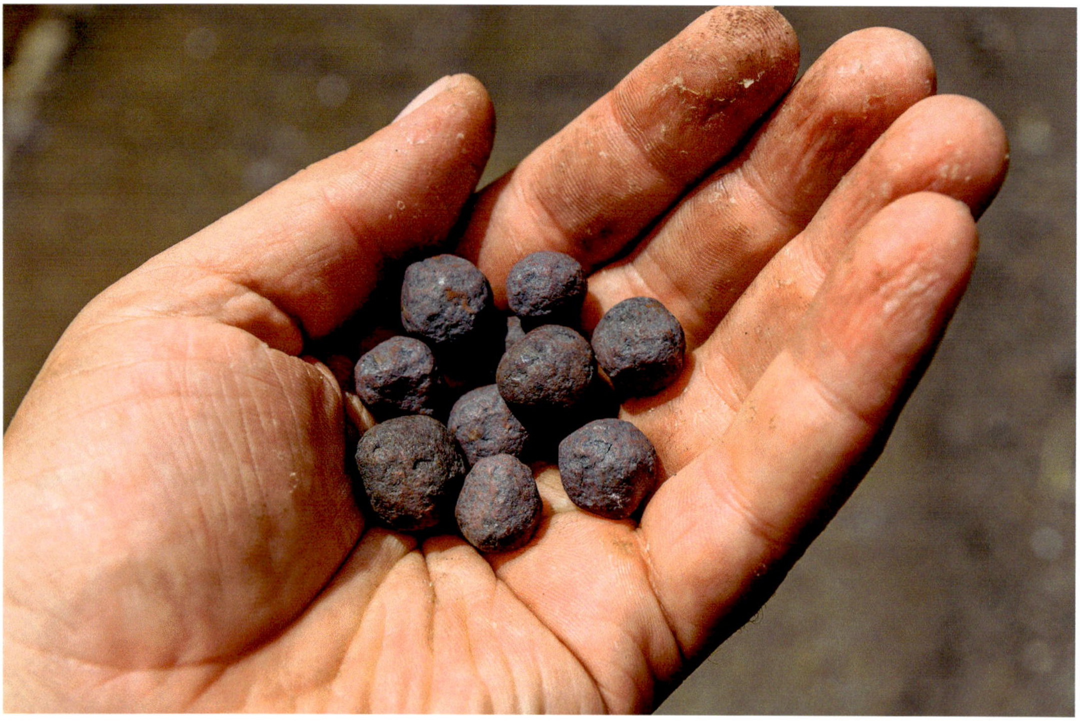

Above: Taconite pellets, a low-grade iron ore. (*photograph credit: Bigstock.com*)

Below left: Coke, the blast furnace's fuel source. (*photograph credit: Bigstock.com*)

Below right: Limestone, which acted as a flux. (*photograph credit: Bigstock.com*)

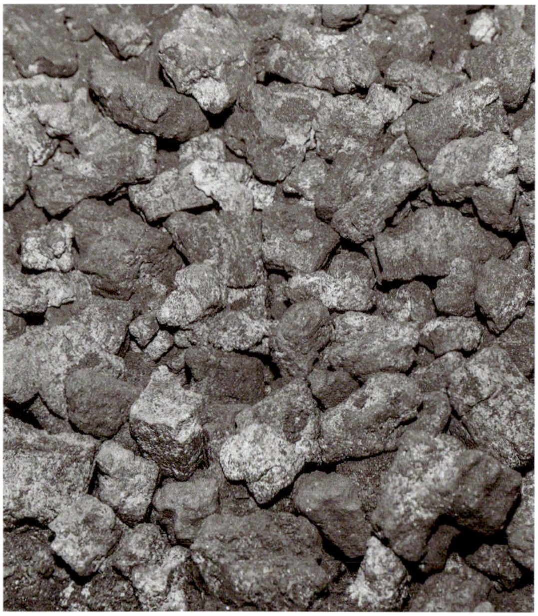

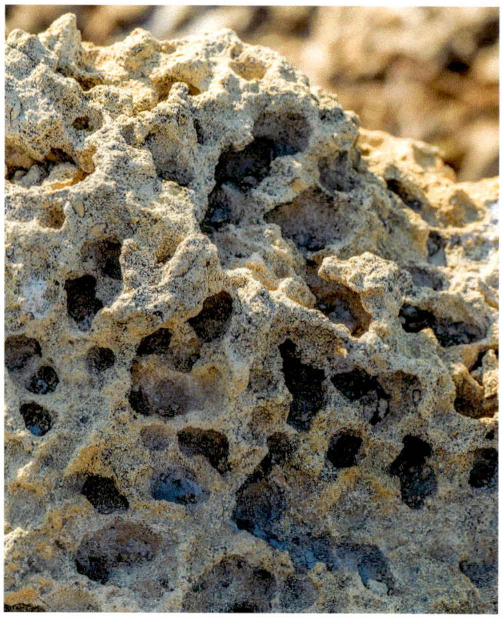

In the blast furnace, the mixture of taconite, coke, and limestone was heated, reducing the taconite to molten "pig iron," named in early days when workers saw a quantity of molten iron run through troughs into ingots, looking to them like a sow with suckling piglets. The pig iron is what gets processed into steel.

Bethlehem Steel used aerial and below-ground geological surveys to determine where productive deposits of taconite and other raw materials were located. In many cases, it then bought the land to mine and quarry the raw materials. Furthering its self-sufficiency, it built the facilities to process the materials to ready them for the blast furnaces. It even owned the short line railroads that brought the stock to its plants. Bethlehem Steel had a strong philosophy of independence, and its autonomy served the company well for many years.

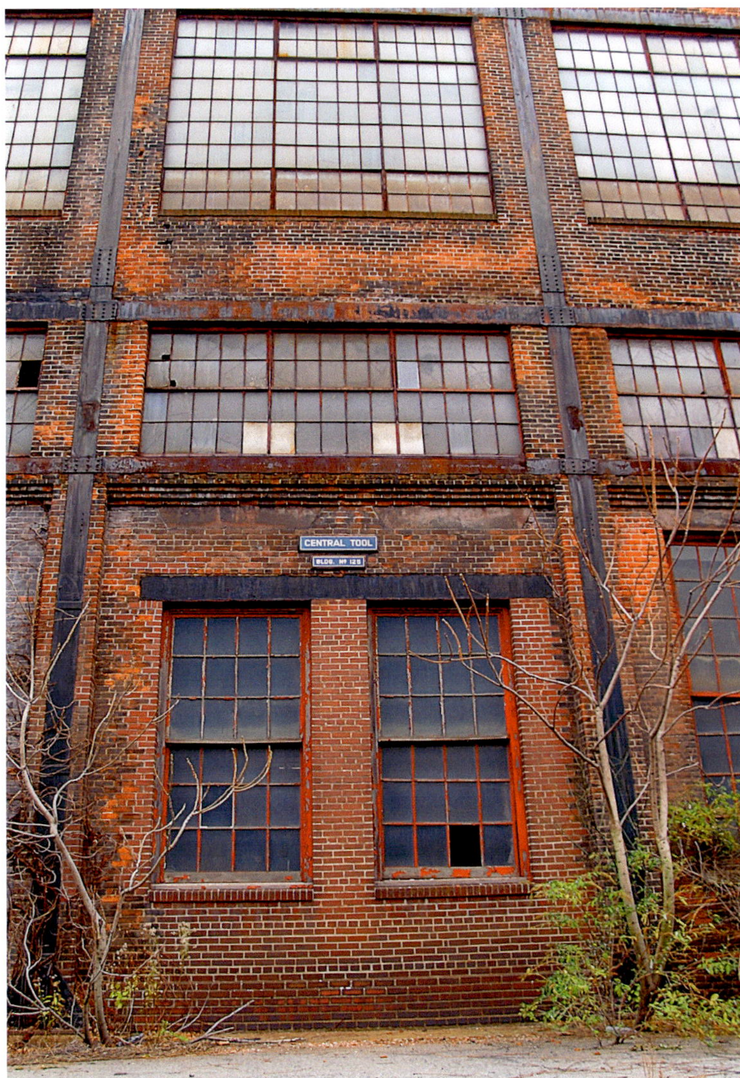

The Central Tool Building. Bethlehem Steel took pride in being largely self-sufficient and fabricated on-site many of the tools required for its operations.

4

THE TRESTLE AND ITS "LARRIES"

In the early days, raw materials were obtained locally and brought to the furnace by horse cart. When iron-making was evolving into production on an industrial scale, two inventors and engineers from Chicago, Frank Hoover and Arthur Mason, were commissioned to design and build a 46-foot-high railroad trestle that bears their name. Self-propelled, bulk material handling cars would run on it, continuously shuttling between where the raw materials were stored, called the "ore yards," and the huge bins in front of each furnace.

Welsh immigrant workers named these 200-ton-capacity railcars "larries," believed to be a pronunciation variation on "lorries," the word for trucks in the United Kingdom. With a cab at each end, the cars could run in either direction. Larries were powered by an electrified overhead wire supported by masts. A pole extended from the edge of the car to contact the wire.

Because of their width and heavy weight, larries ran on rails 7 feet 10½ inches apart called "broad gauge." The trestle also had standard-gauge trackage with rails 4 feet 8½ inches apart to bring in loaded railroad hopper cars, use of which was especially important if larries were inoperable. Blast furnaces could not be allowed to cool unless intentionally taken offline for cleaning or repair.

After dumping their load into the bins, the larry operator got out of the front cab, lowered the back pole, raised the front pole to contact the overhead wire, and from the back cab ran the car to the ore yards for more material. Like so many functions at Bethlehem Steel, the cars ran 24/7 in a "just-in-time" operation, long before such terms became common expressions.

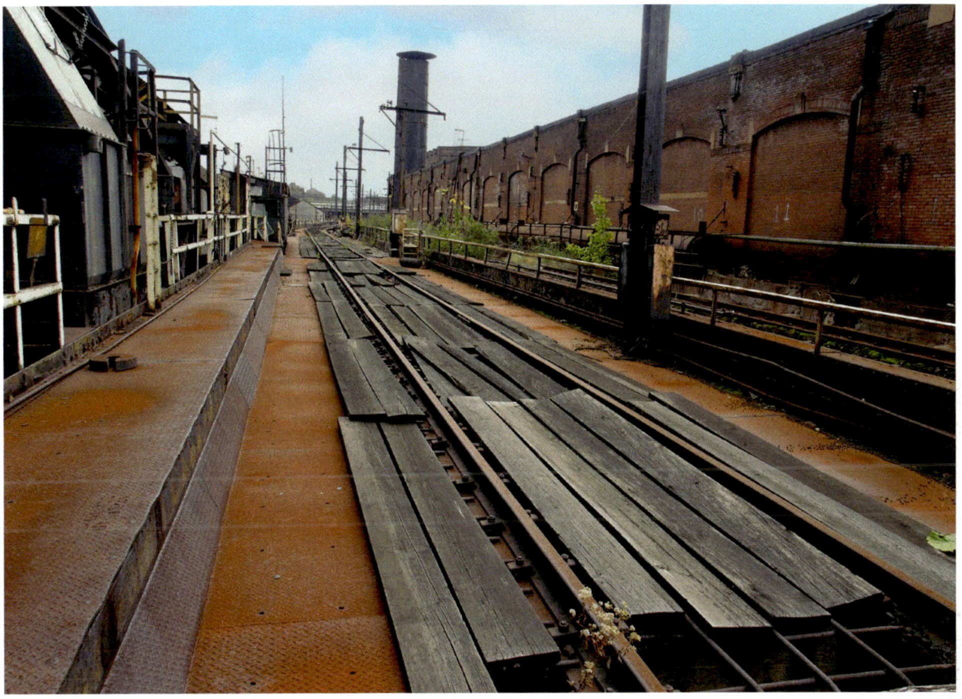

A section of abandoned trestle, later retrofitted with a fenced pedestrian walkway (not shown) for tourists. The brickwork of the Gas Blowing Engine House appears on the right.

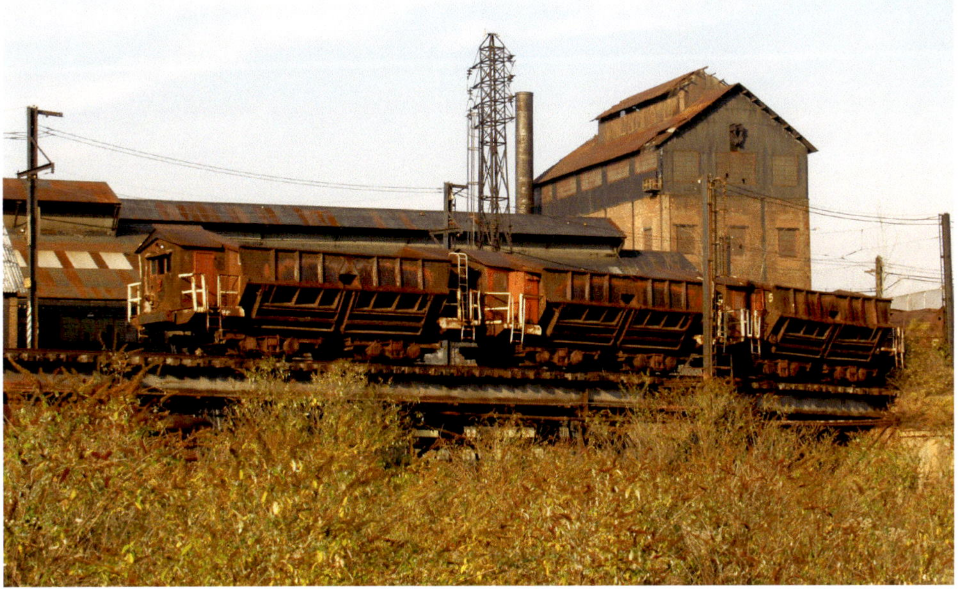

Three abandoned "larries" await their fate on the trestle. The vertical heat treatment High House appears notably in the background.

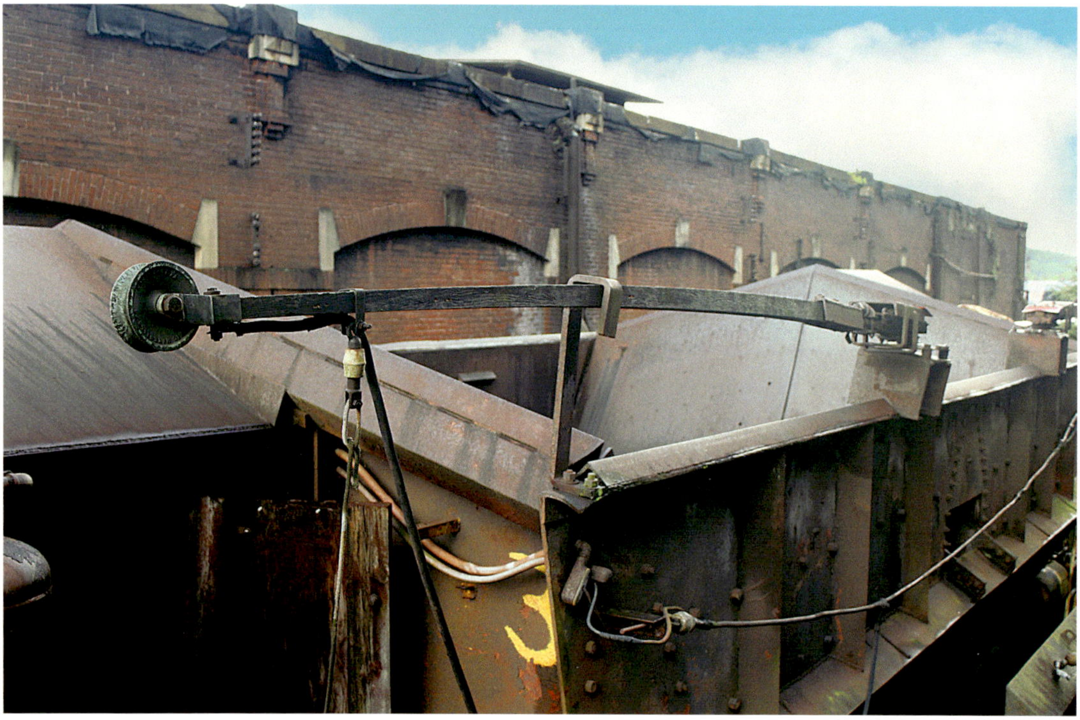

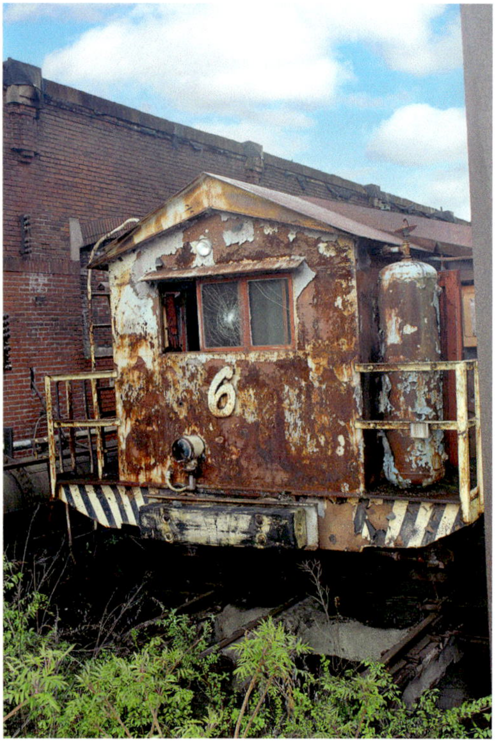

Above: This intact pole on Larry Car #3 would be raised to contact the electrified overhead wire. Photograph taken in 2023.

Left: Larry Car #6. Photograph taken in 2023.

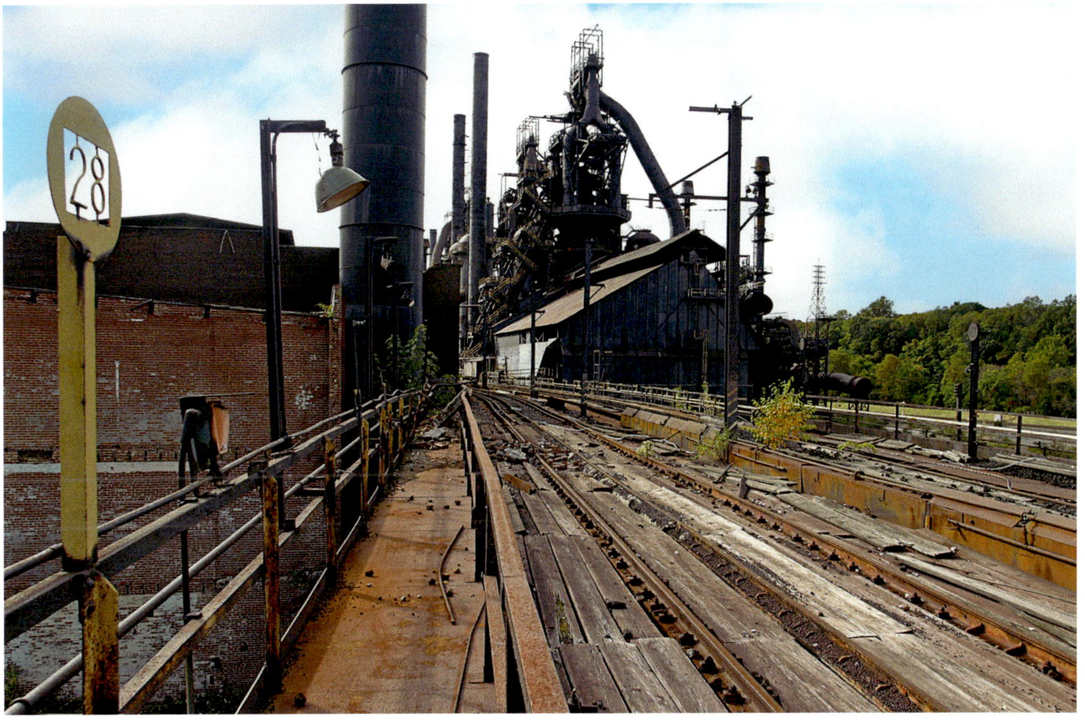

Above: A section of derelict trestle with blast furnaces in the background. Blast Furnace E appears first in the lineup.

Right: Looking down a heavily patinaed ladder to the Hoover-Mason Trestle below.

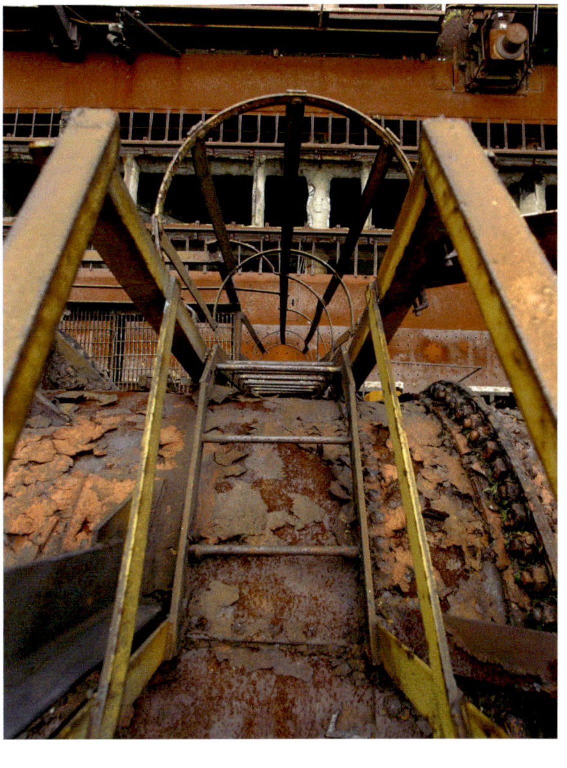

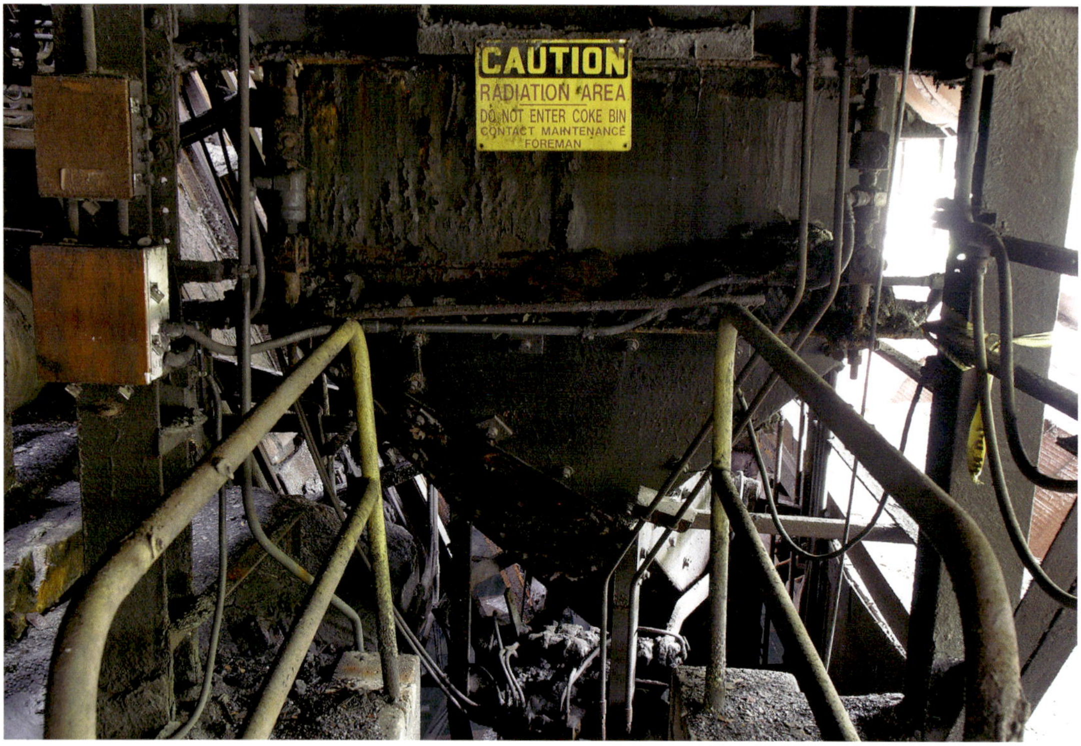

Above: Coke bin posted with a radiation caution sign.

Below left: A danger sign for the bins. Dynamiting was sometimes used in the winter to loosen frozen ore.

Below right: A caution sign warns of pellets being dumped by the larry cars from the trestle above. The imagery shows a worker being barraged by the cascade of pellets.

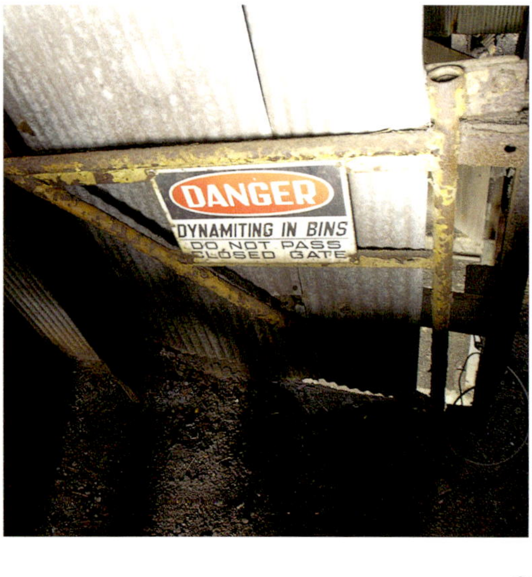

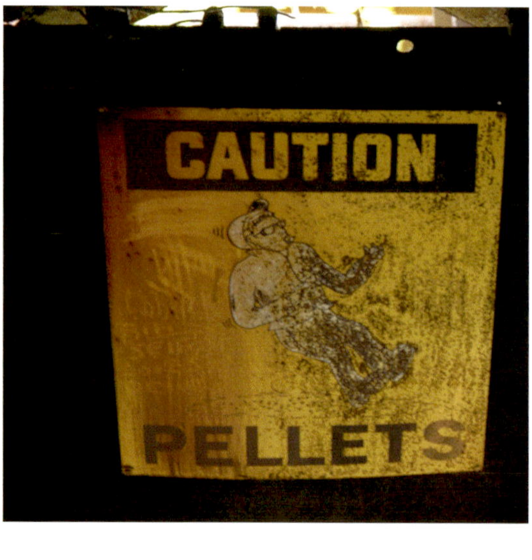

5

SCALE CARS AND SKIP CARS

The blast furnaces required exact ratios of taconite, coke, and limestone from the bins. Scale cars, or weigh cars, powered by an electrified, overhead third rail, ran in the darkness below the trestle, weighing the raw materials. To make a ton of iron, the approximate ratio was 2 tons of taconite, 1 ton of coke, and ½ ton of limestone, although Bethlehem Steel used precise weights to make a consistent quality product.

After weighing, funicular-like cars, sometimes called "skip tubs," were loaded with what the workers called "the burden" and pulled up a steep "skip hoist" incline to the furnace top, where the material was dumped into the furnace through a "charge hopper." The cars ran on two parallel tracks and were counterbalanced by each other: One loaded car went up as the other empty one came down. Before there were any scale cars or skip cars, it took the muscle power of strong men to load wheelbarrows with the right recipe of iron ore, limestone, and charcoal to feed the furnace.

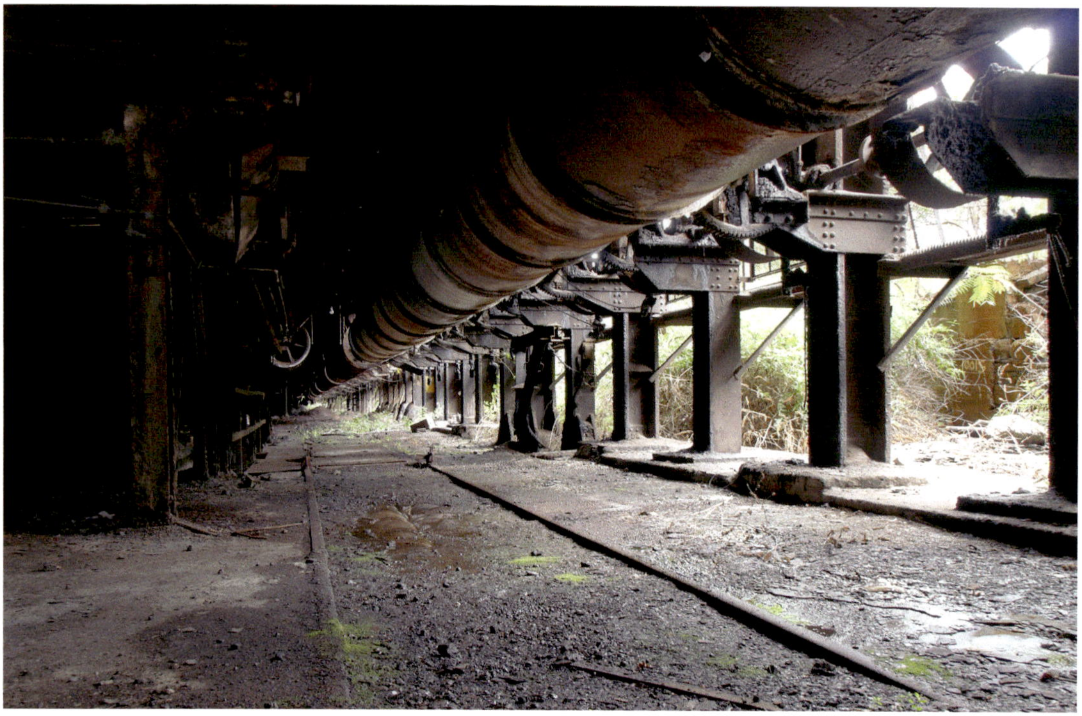

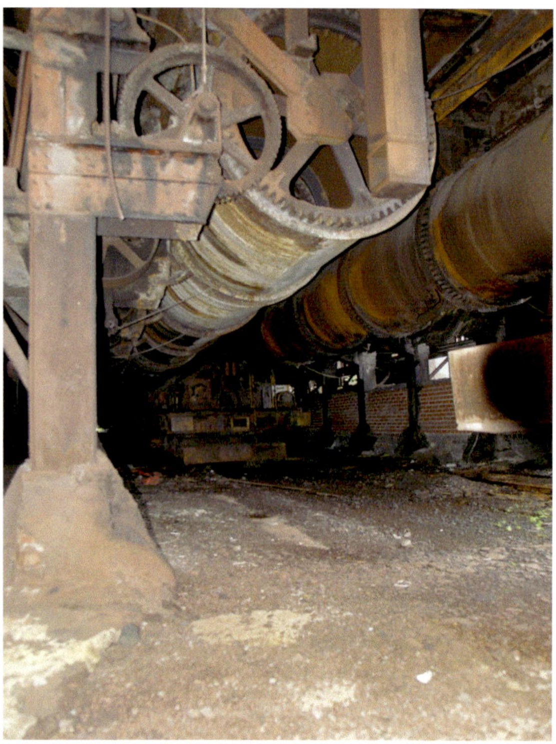

Above: Scale car railroad track below the Hoover-Mason Trestle. The low overhead clearance here is readily apparent.

Left: Abandoned Scale Car #11 (center of photograph) lies in the gloom below the trestle.

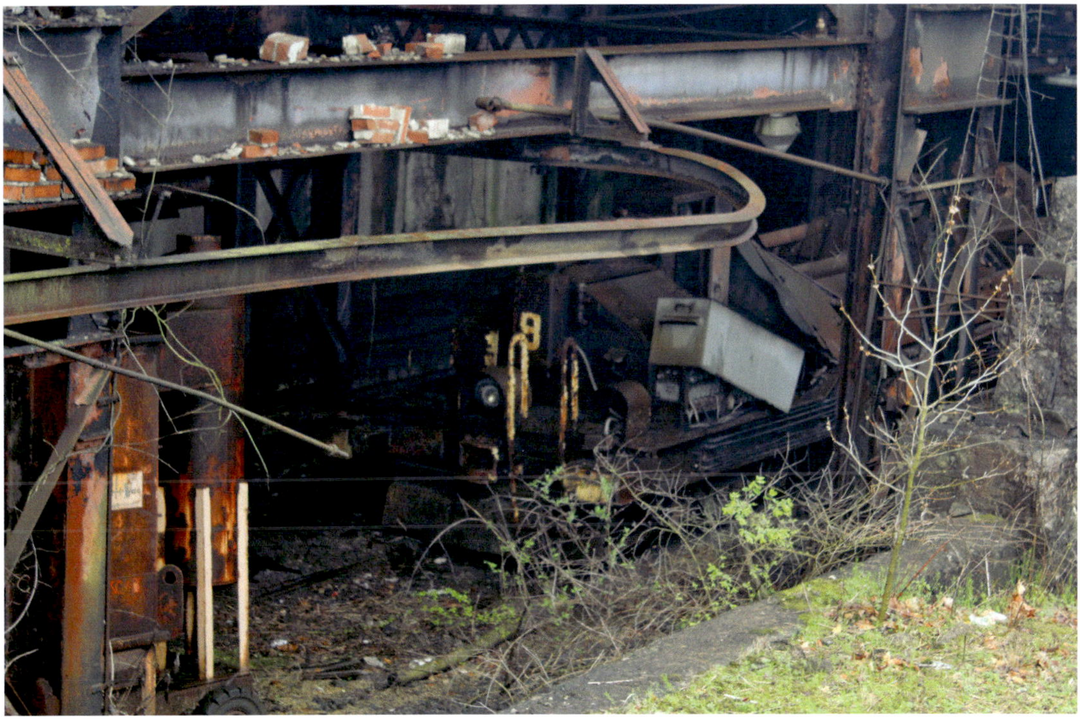

Above: Deteriorating Scale Car #9. Photograph taken in 2023.

Right: A section of scale car railroad track that is uncharacteristically flooded with natural light. The electrified feed rail for the scale cars appears overhead.

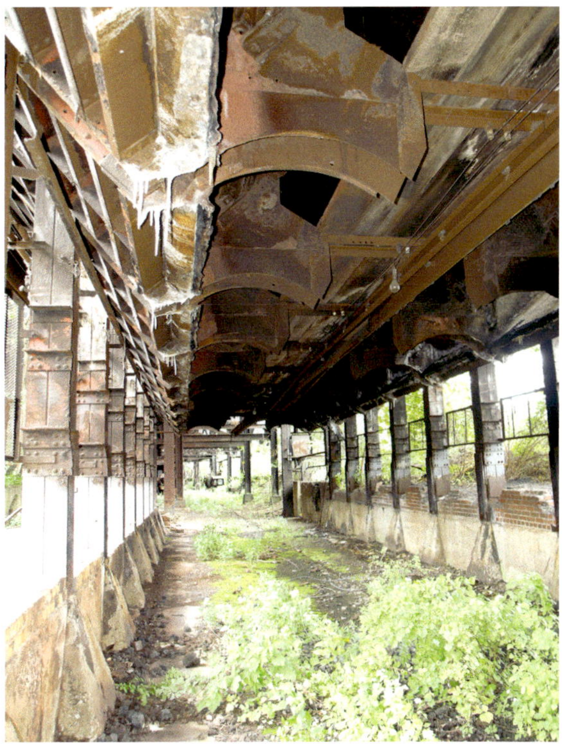

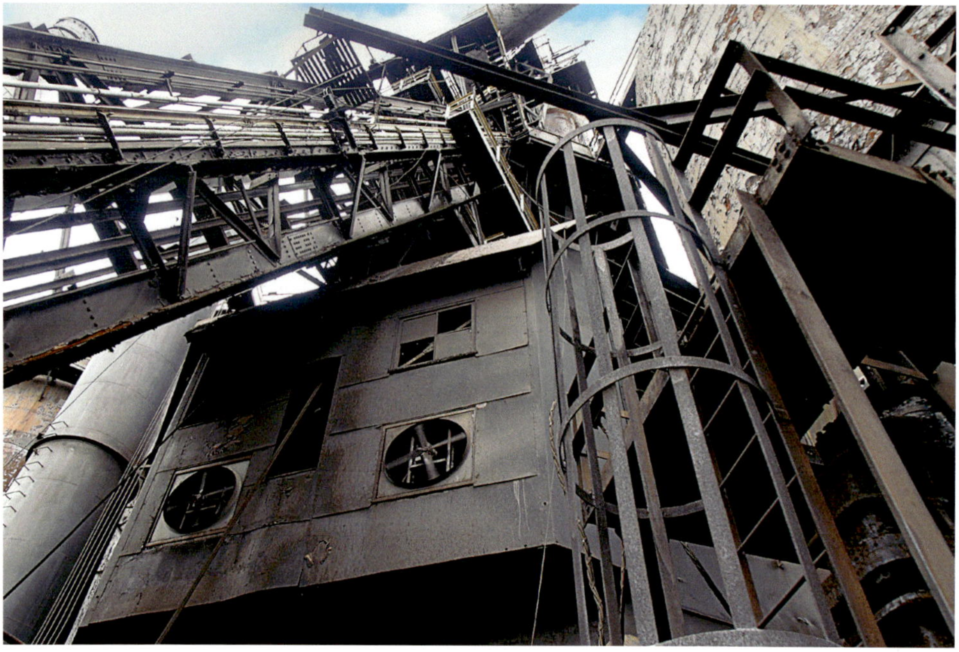

A skip hoist track appears on the left as it steeply ascends toward the top of a blast furnace. On the day I took this photograph, the wind caused both fans in the lower left to eerily rotate as if the plant was somehow still operational.

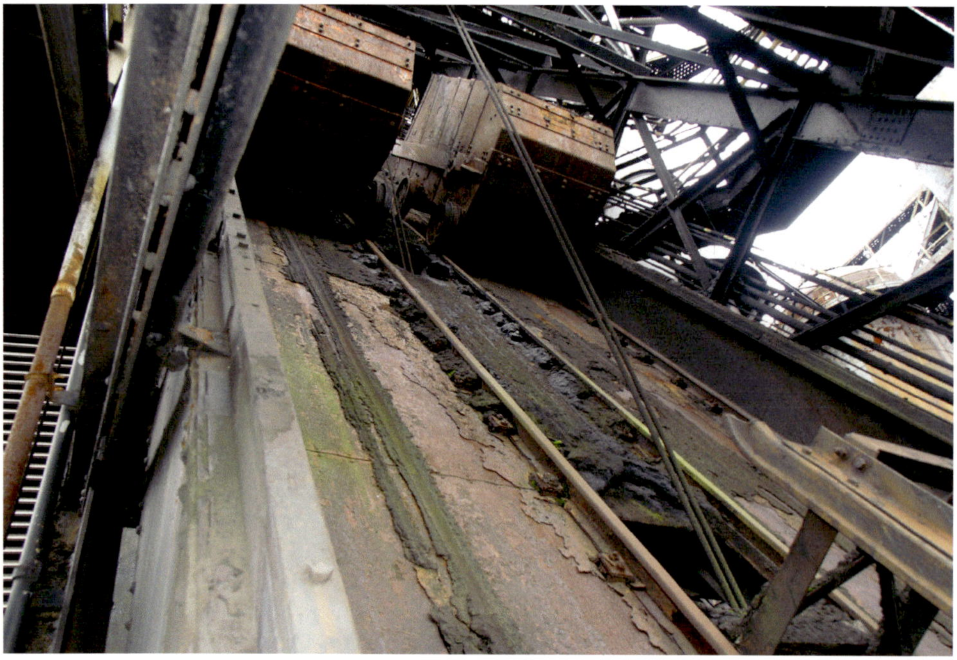

Skip cars on the skip hoist track.

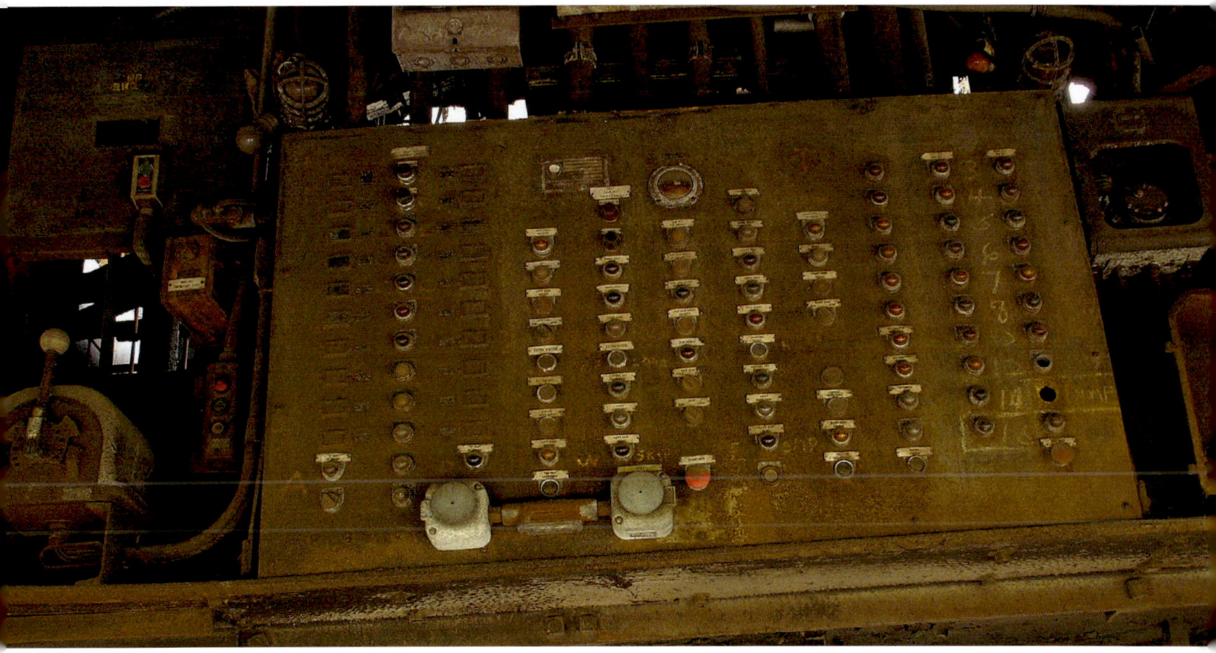

A control panel for the skip cars.

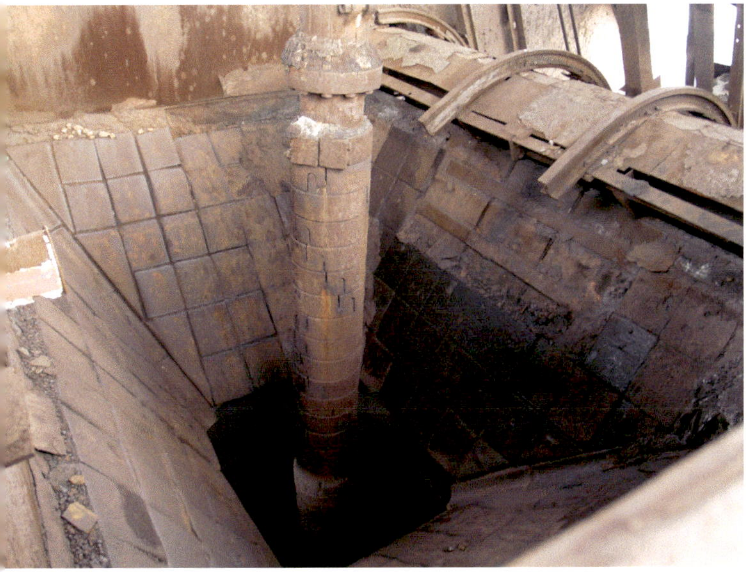

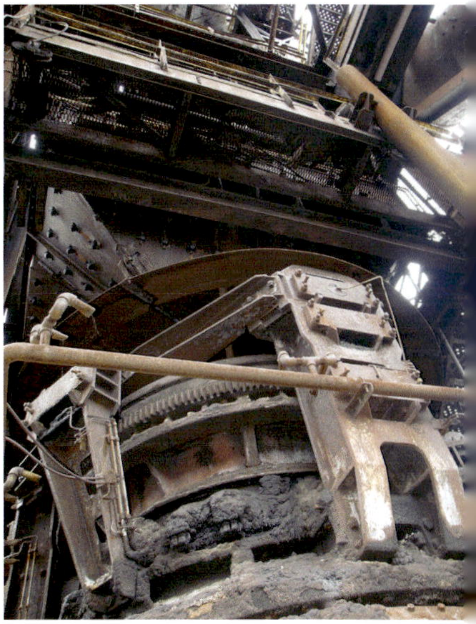

Above left: At the top of the skip hoist track, skip cars would follow the curved rail as they tip to empty their burden of raw material into the charge hopper.

Above right: Looking up at the throat of the charge hopper for Blast Furnace D.

6

THE BLAST FURNACES

The most iconic symbols of a steel mill are the blast furnaces. The Bethlehem plant at one time had seven of them. Inside the furnaces, coke was burned to achieve a temperature of approximately 3,000 degrees Fahrenheit to smelt taconite into molten iron for processing into steel. A blast furnace is a vessel within a vessel. The outside is steel, but the inside is lined with refractory brick that can withstand the heat of the molten iron and prevent it from touching the outside metal to which it would quickly fuse.

A first-generation operating furnace, now long gone, was on the property as far back as 1863 when the oldest remaining building, known as the Stock House and today a visitor center, had the raw materials of iron-making lying ready on its floor. Furnace A, presently the oldest in "blast furnace row," was completed in 1904, rebuilt in 1950, and not used beyond 1960. It is the only furnace with riveted seams; the other furnaces have welded seams. Furnaces B and D are the largest, reaching nearly 250 feet high, and each capable of producing up to 3,000 tons of iron a day. Furnace C was the last to make iron at the Bethlehem plant in an emotional ceremony in November 1995. Furnace E is the newest of the remaining furnaces and the one with two skip cars, side by side, clearly visible on the steep inclined railway. Furnaces F and G were severely damaged during cleaning in March 1948, when water was sprayed in a furnace that had not sufficiently cooled, resulting in a deadly explosion. Never rebuilt, they were dismantled in the 1960s.

The furnaces at the Bethlehem plant were considered small when contrasted with Bethlehem Steel's last furnace, built in the late 1970s at the company's Sparrows Point, Maryland, plant, which could produce 8,000 tons of iron each day.

Inside the furnace, the burning coke creates carbon monoxide, which reduces the chemical compound of iron and oxygen, called iron oxide, into molten iron. The concept of using a furnace to make molten iron likely came from what is now China as early as the first century. In the west, the early Romans smelted iron in furnaces, and the concept flourished across Europe during the Middle Ages and the Industrial Revolution.

Three or more silo-like structures called "stoves" stand adjacent to each furnace, providing a flow of heated compressed air that is blown into the furnace through

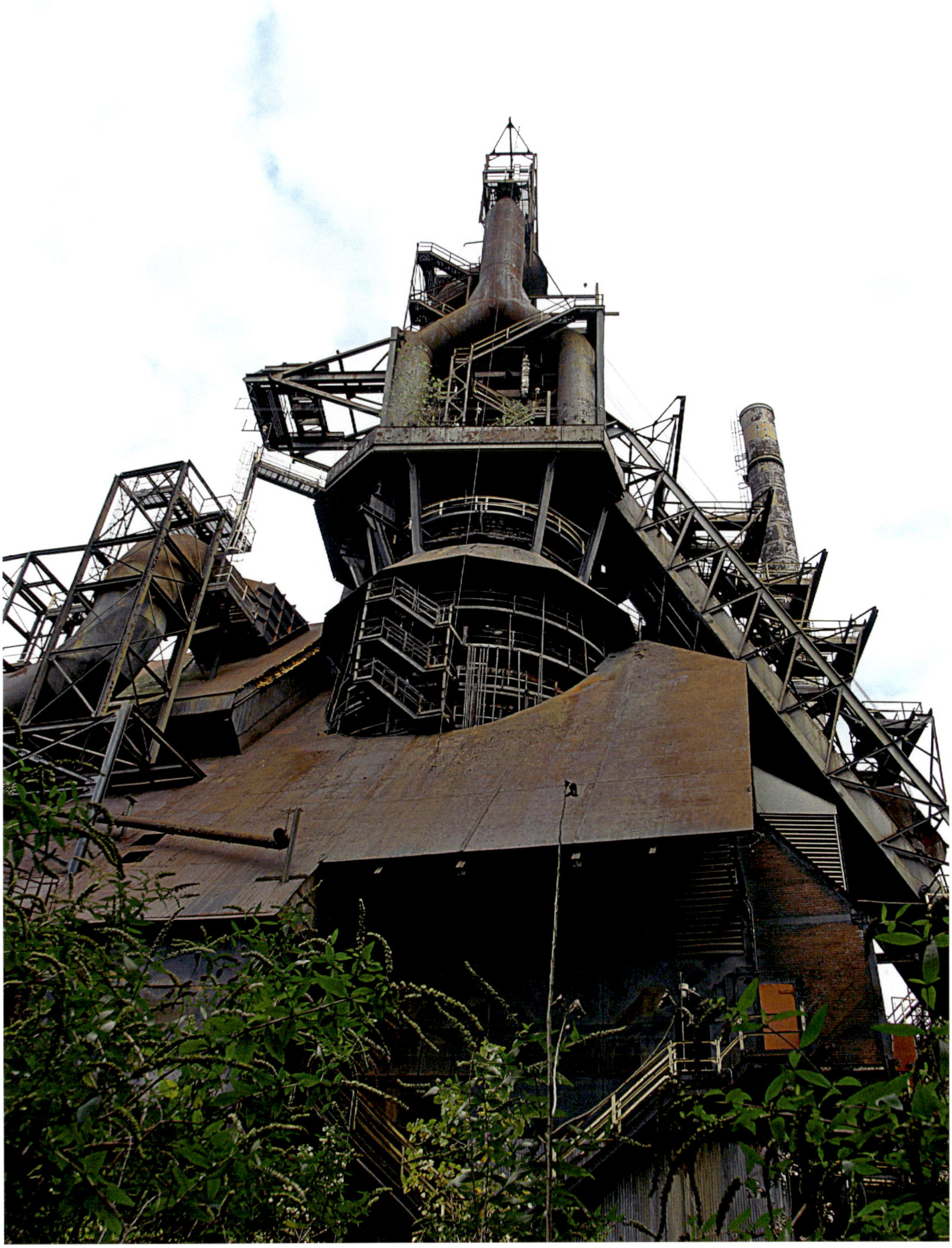

This blast furnace towers nearly 250 feet high. The skip cars would ride up the angled skip hoist track on the right. The overgrown vegetation reaches for the rust-hued cast house roof.

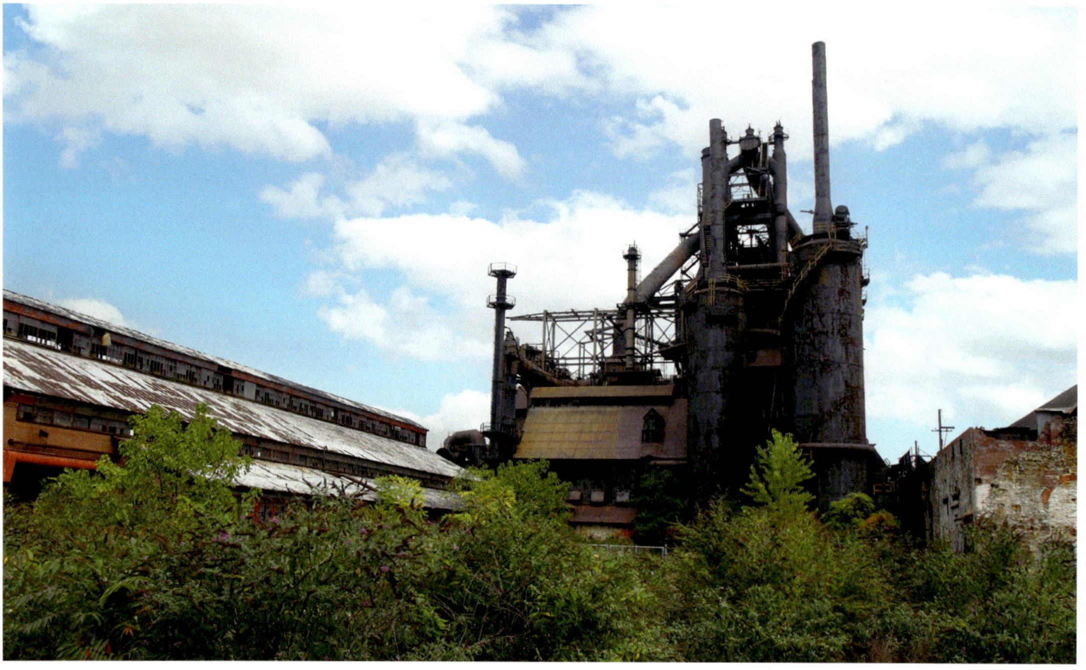

Blast Furnace A. The Turn & Grind Shop appears on the left, and the Stock House (now rebuilt as the Southside Visitor Center) appears on the right.

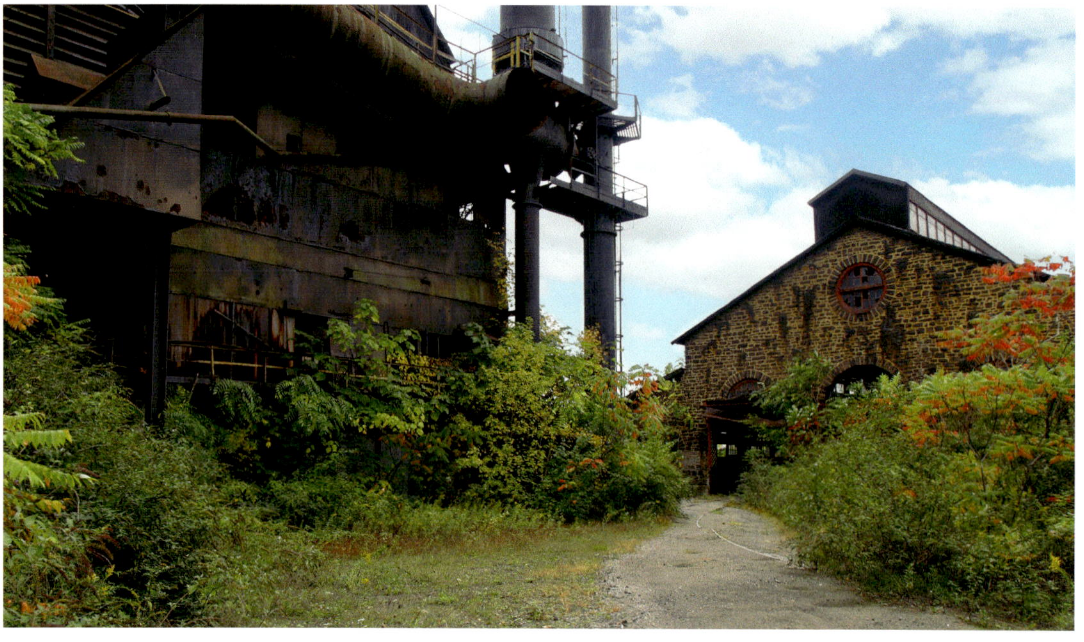

The old stone end wall and round "rose" window of the Turn & Grind Shop is partially hidden by overgrowth. The base of Blast Furnace A looms large on the left.

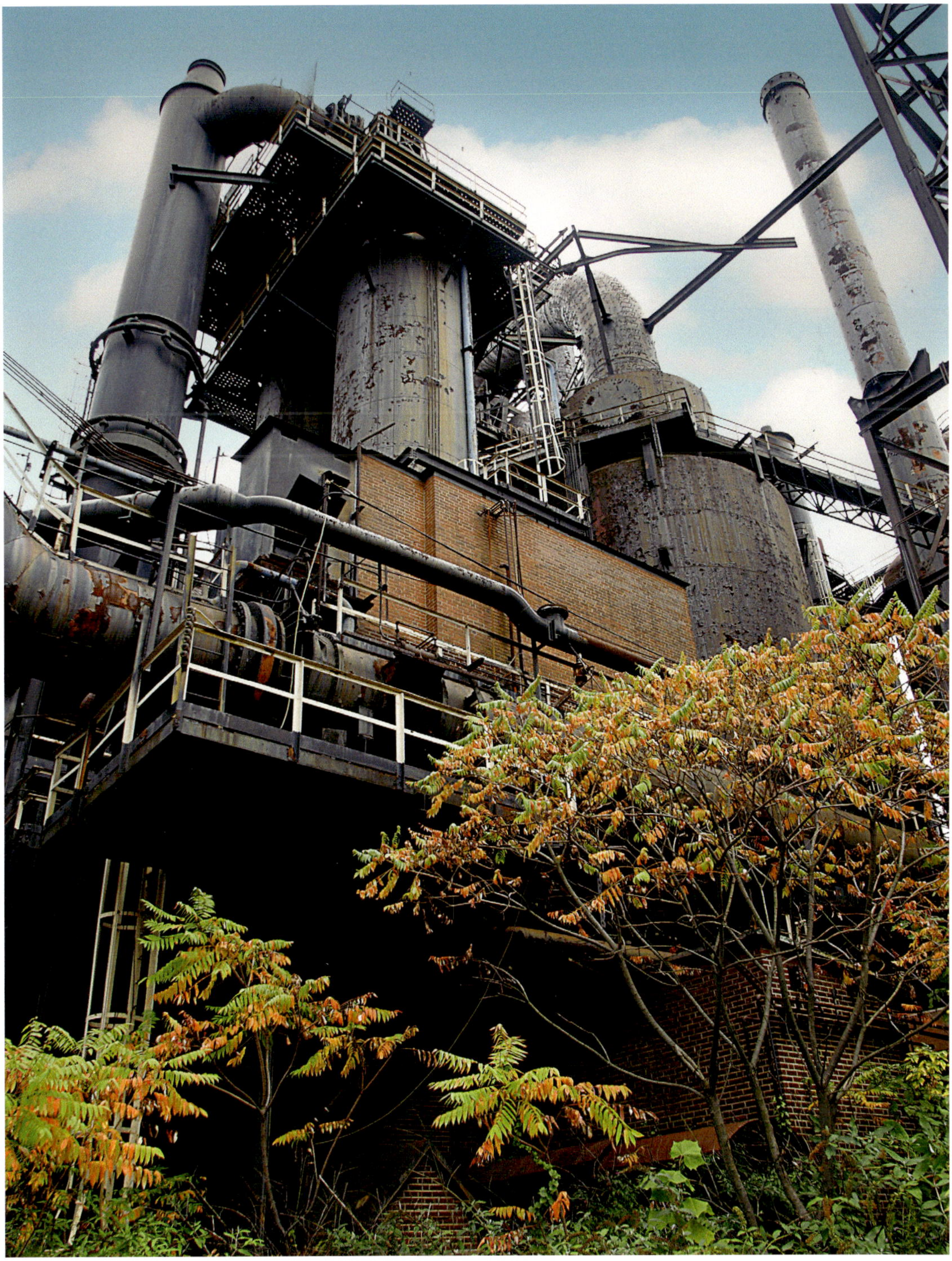

Blast Furnace A, dating to 1904.

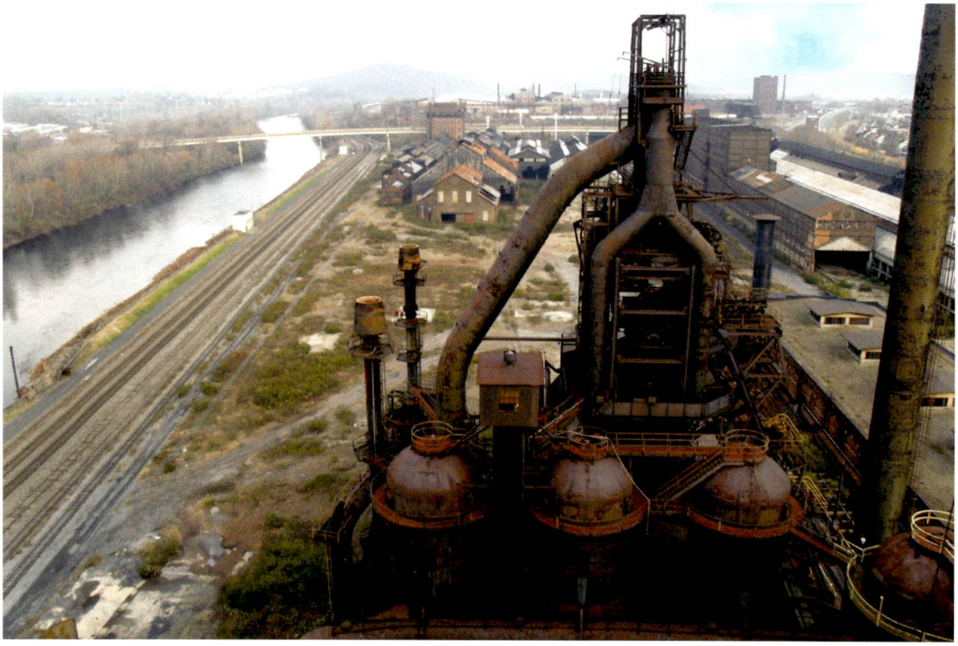

Blast Furnace E. The open field in the middle of the photograph is where Blast Furnaces F and G formerly stood.

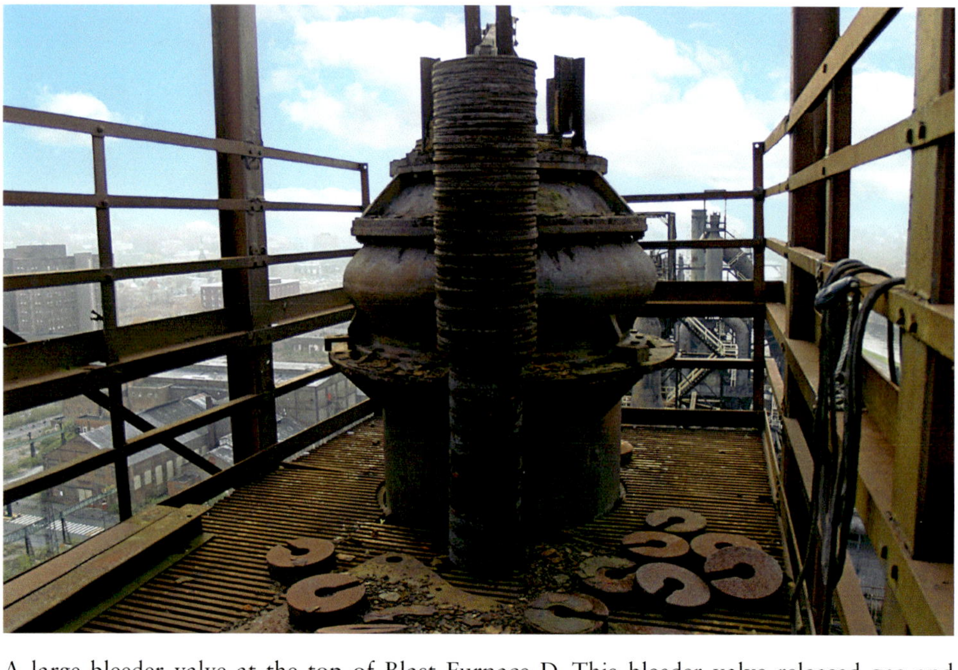

A large bleeder valve at the top of Blast Furnace D. This bleeder valve released gas and pressure when necessary. The weight plates acted as counterweights and allowed fine-tuning of the valve opening and closing action.

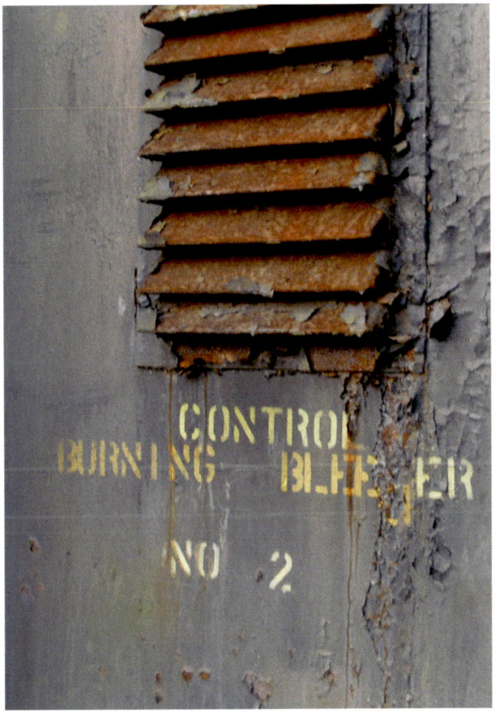

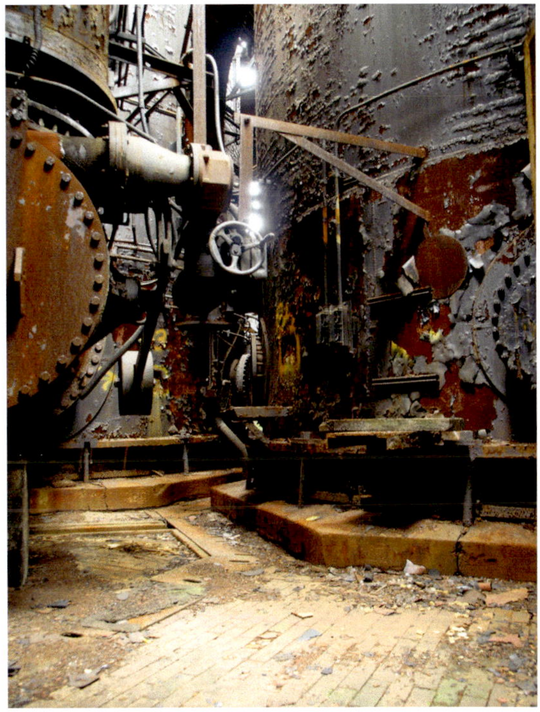

Above left: Access door to a burning bleeder control. Bleeder valves for releasing pressure were vital to the plant operations.

Above right: A scene of flaking paint and rusting metal along "blast furnace row."

nozzles, called tuyeres, at the bottom of the fire to keep the chemical reaction continuing evenly throughout the entire furnace. The forced air also makes the fire hotter, like blowing on a campfire or using a bellows on a home fireplace. This injection of air into the furnace is why they are called blast furnaces.

Bethlehem Pennsylvania's blast furnaces were prominently featured in the opening sequence of the 2009 action movie *Transformers: Revenge of the Fallen*.

During iron-making, a lighter waste product called slag separates and rises to the top of the molten iron. Slag is largely comprised of the impurities from the iron ore, and in floating on the surface of the hot liquid, it serves to control the temperature of the mixture in the furnace. Slag is periodically removed and put into specialized railroad cars. The slag cars, called "cinder pots" by the workers, were taken to the slag dump, where the cars were tipped, dumping the hot liquid down a hillside. When cooled, the molten slag fuses into a hard, glassy material that can be broken into pieces.

While much of the slag that steel mills create simply goes to waste, some becomes an ingredient in cement and is used as part of the material to make asphalt road surfaces and airport tarmacs. It is also used as an ingredient in fertilizer and even as an aggregate for landscaping.

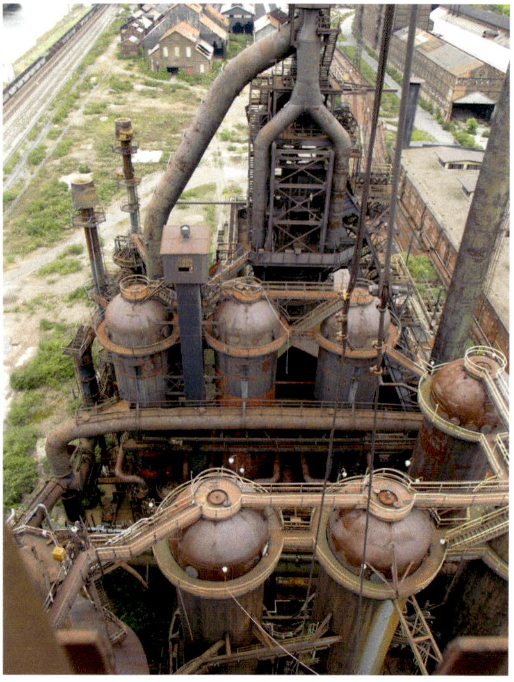

Left: Stoves to support the hot blast air injection into the blast furnace.

Below: A well-worn armchair caked in dust provides reference of scale on this blast furnace cast floor. While partially covered by other piping, the massive bustle pipe that feeds the tuyeres is evident in the upper left. The bustle pipe forms a complete ring around the blast furnace.

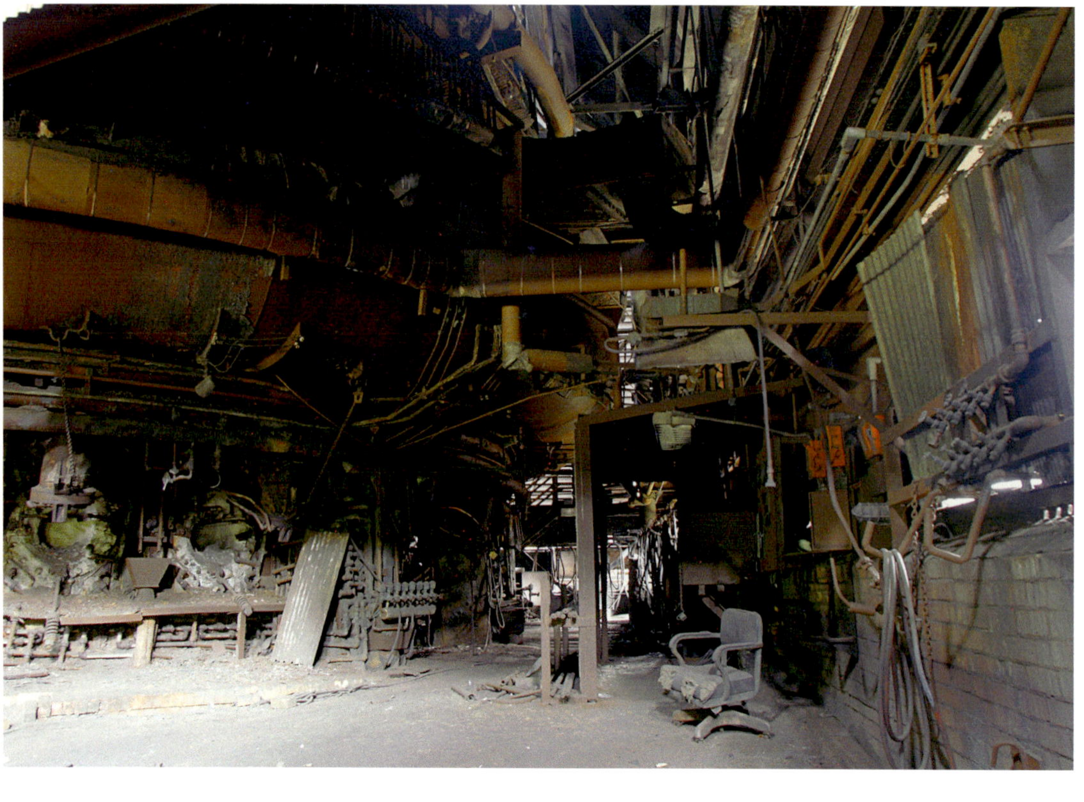

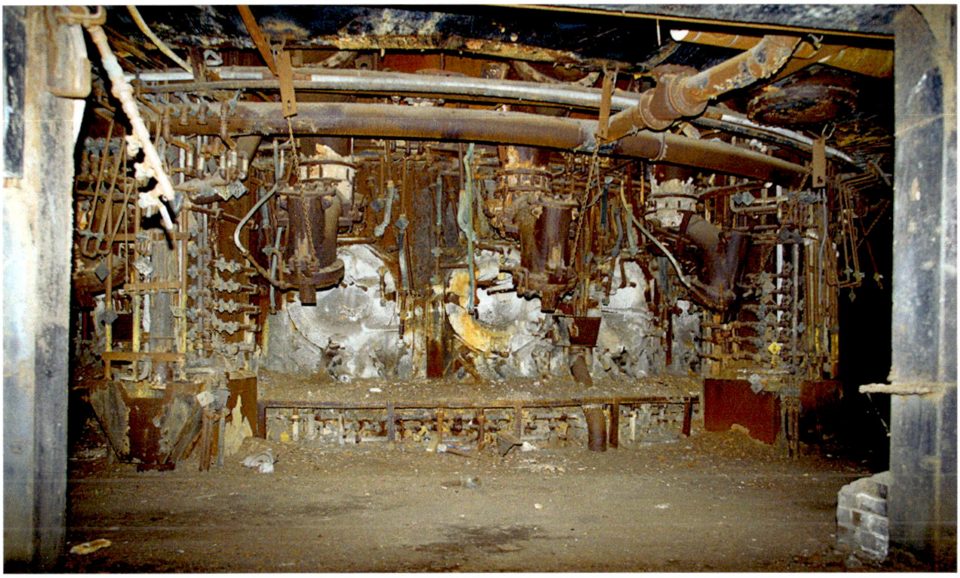

Three tuyeres wait to be swung into position to blast hot air into the blast furnace. This would occur just above the hearth of the blast furnace, where the molten material would ultimately be tapped.

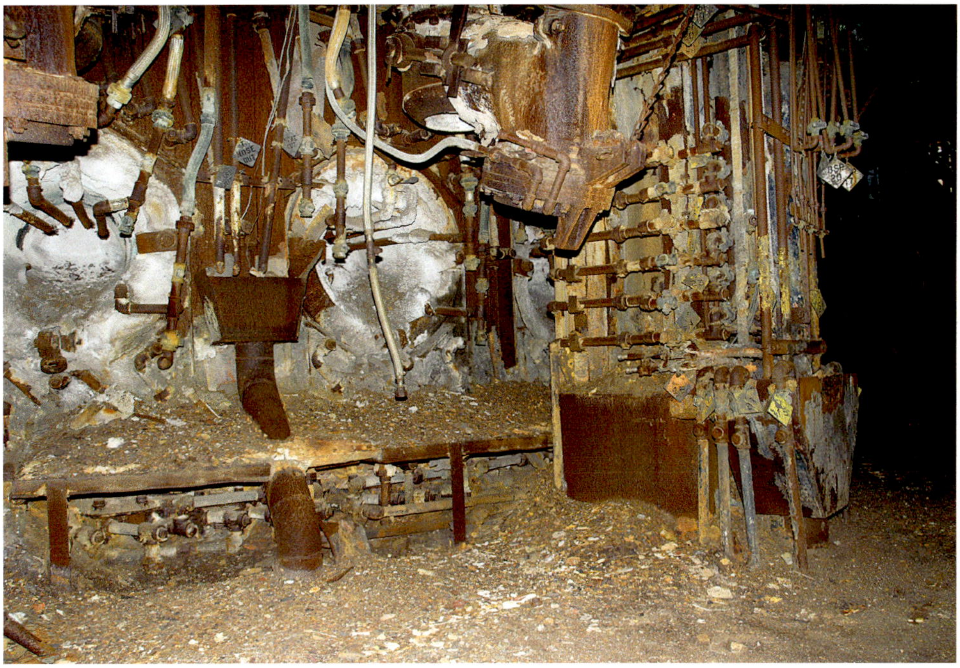

A close-up showing a raised tuyere. The numerous smaller pipes were used for cooling the area immediately around the tuyere to prevent the tuyere itself from melting due to the extreme temperatures inside an operational blast furnace.

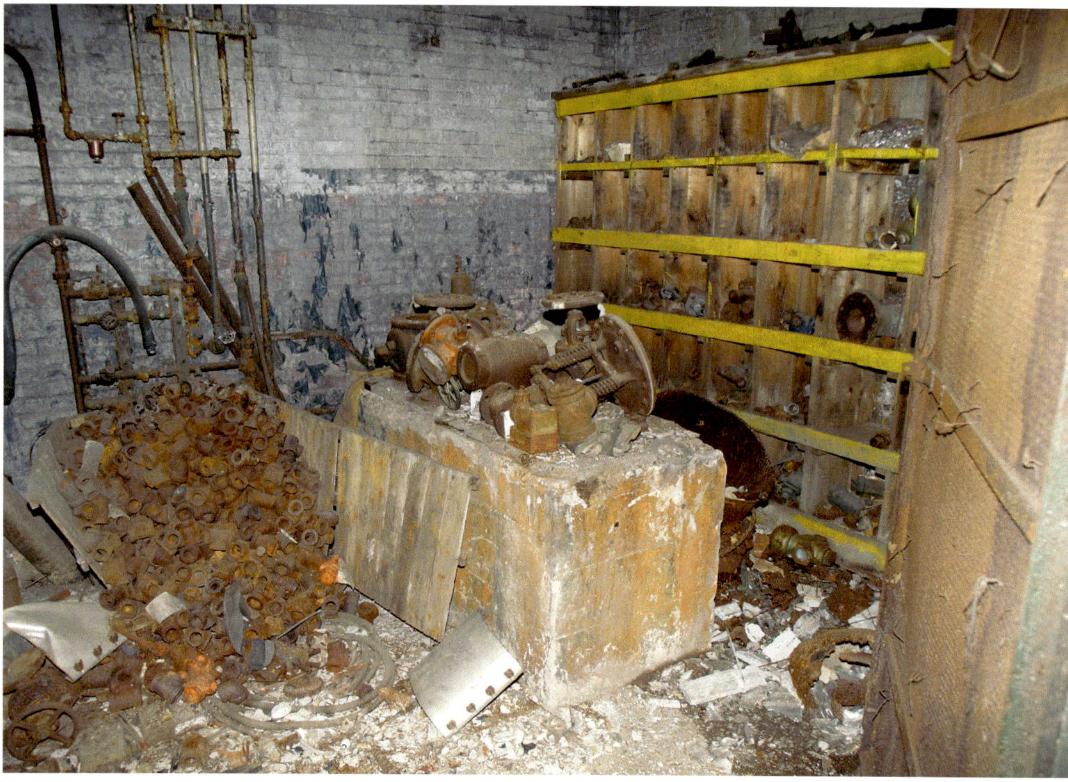

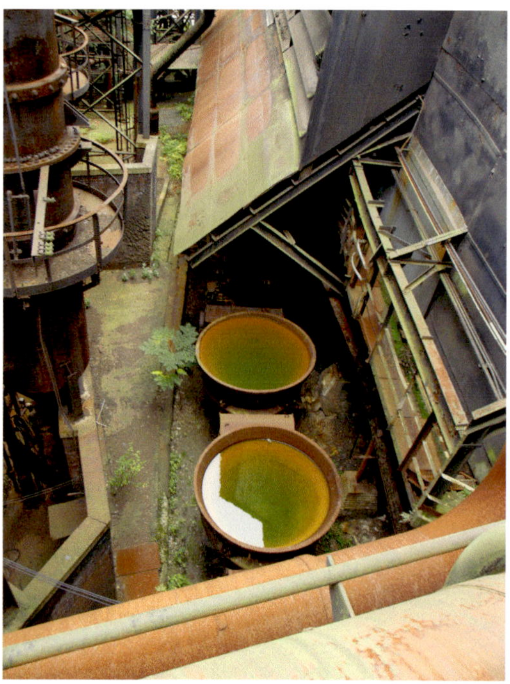

Above: Plumbing fittings intended for blast furnace repairs.

Left: Looking from above into a disused slag railroad car filled with rainwater.

7

MAKING IRON INTO STEEL

The blast furnaces were periodically tapped, called "casting." It was done by creating a tap hole into the furnace hearth, permitting the molten iron to run down troughs in the cast floor to waiting, specialized hot metal railcars, nicknamed "subs" because they looked like submarines, but also called "torpedo" or "bottle" cars. Sometimes these cars carried the hot pig iron to a foundry to make products of cast iron, but mostly the destination was the basic oxygen furnace (BOF), where oxygen was forced through the liquid iron to remove impurities, sulfur, phosphorus, and excess carbon by the basic oxygen method. This reduced impurities from about 4½ percent to between ½ and 1½ percent. In simple terms, this is the point at which iron becomes raw steel, making it less brittle and four to six times stronger than iron. In the 1960s, the BOF method superseded the open-hearth process, which had evolved from the original Bessemer process. All of these methods had the same goal of removing impurities from the iron to convert it to steel.

The addition of other elements to the steel, including nickel, chromium, manganese, and vanadium, makes an alloy. An alloy is formed when combining another element (metal or nonmetal) with a metal.

In earlier days, the next step was pouring the hot liquid into ingots. Henry Grey (1849–1913), a British-born steelmaker, conceived of making a structural beam from passing a single ingot through a series of rollers instead of riveting together overlapped smaller beams. The continuously rolled wide flange beam became the industry standard for steel framework construction. It was strong, yet used minimal material. Known as the Bethlehem beam, it revolutionized structural steel.

Beginning in the 1950s, pouring molten steel into ingots was replaced by continuous casting. The process used a large reservoir called a tundish that is constantly supplied with molten steel, releasing it through tubes to produce long steel strands of indeterminate length. Continuous casting saved time, improved consistency, and increased worker productivity.

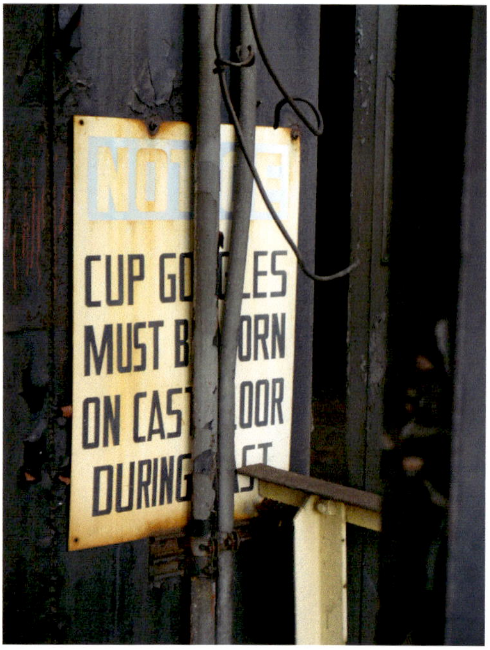

Left: A sign indicates that cup goggles must be worn on the cast floor during casting.

Below: A blast furnace cast floor. The hearth of the blast furnace appears toward the middle/top of the photograph. It is here that the furnace would be tapped. The vertical steel guard positioned there would help protect the workers from the heat and fury of the active tap hole. The troughs would direct the molten material as it flowed out of the blast furnace.

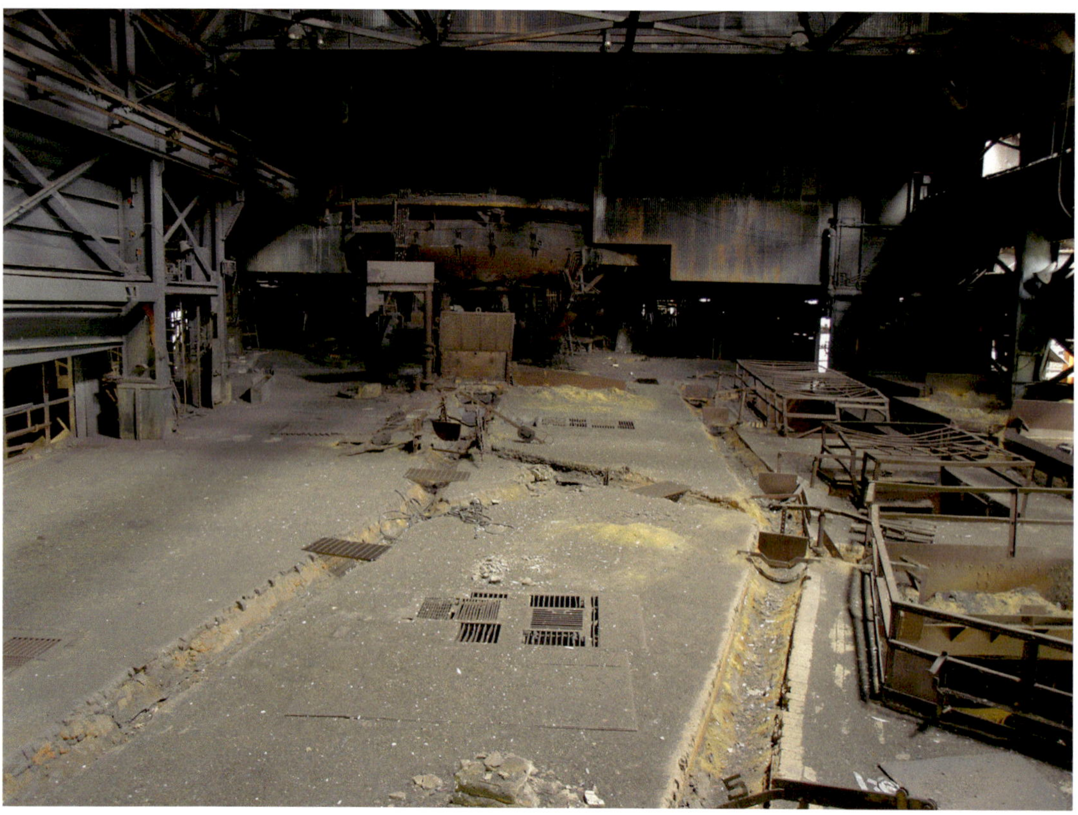

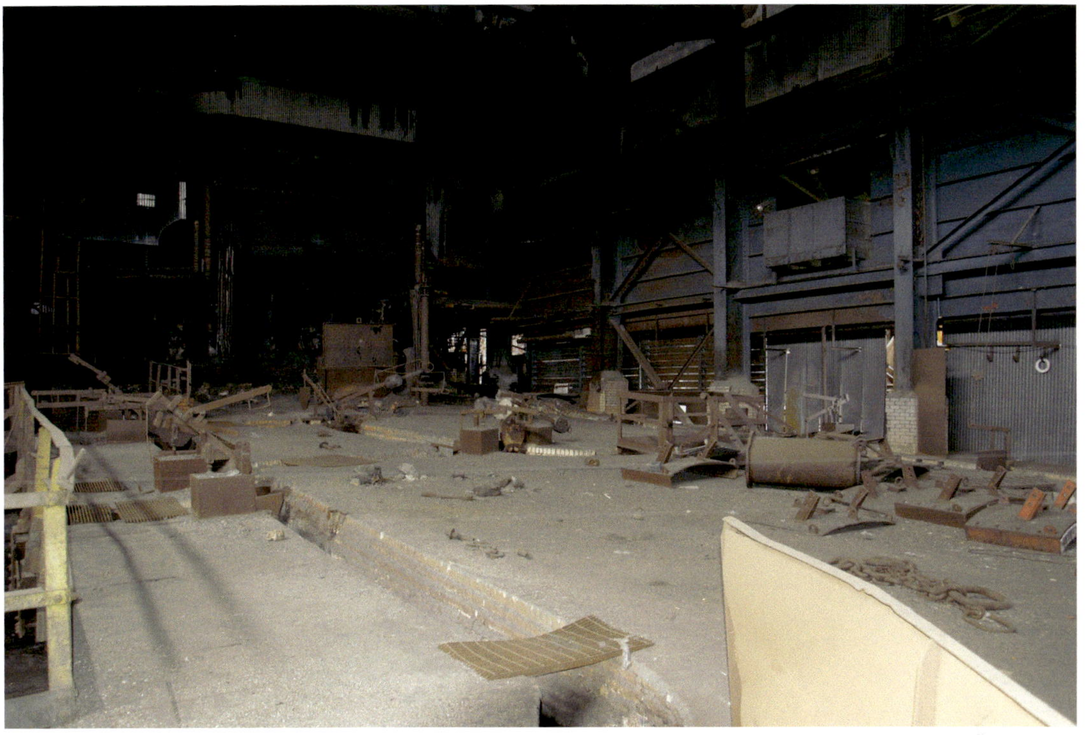

A blast furnace cast floor and trough lined with refractory brick.

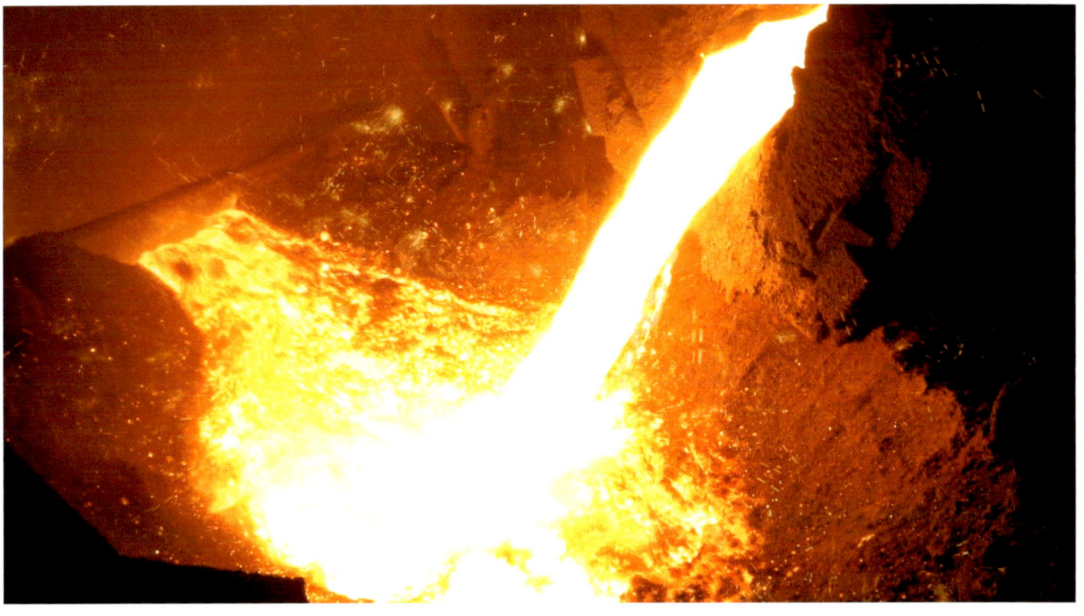

Smelting at an unidentified steel plant. Molten metal and slag would flow out of a tap hole into the troughs. (*photograph credit: Bigstock.com*)

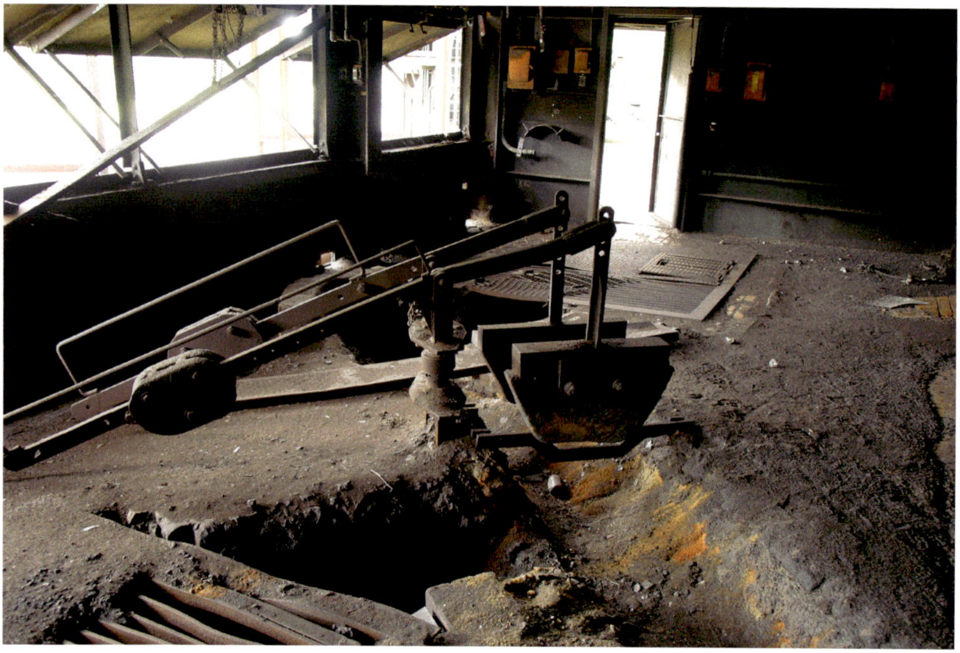

Cast floor trough detail showing where the molten material would be directed into the railroad cars waiting below.

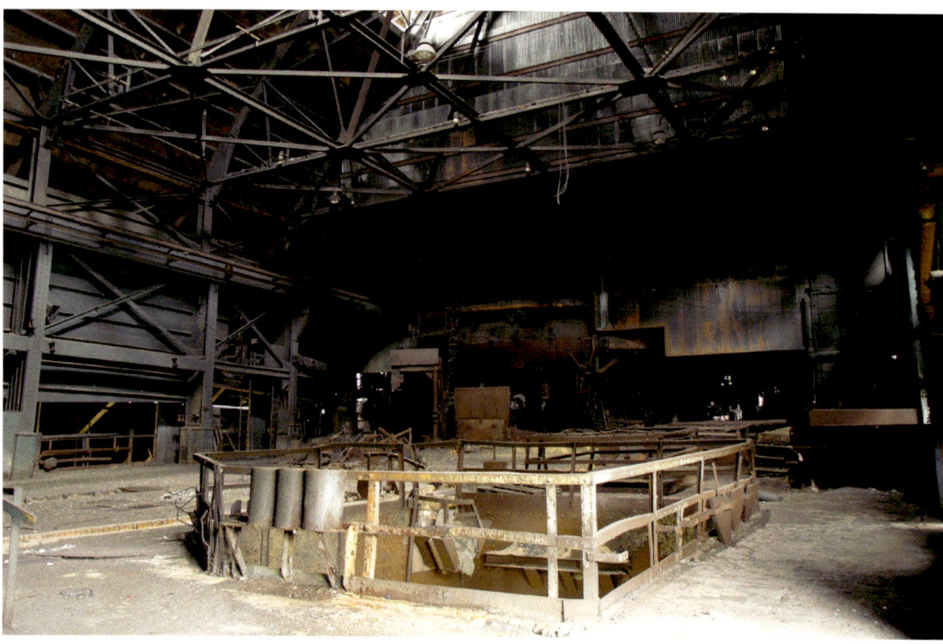

The big expanse of a cast house with another view of where the molten material would exit a cast floor trough (visible in the middle of the yellow railing) before dropping into a railroad car.

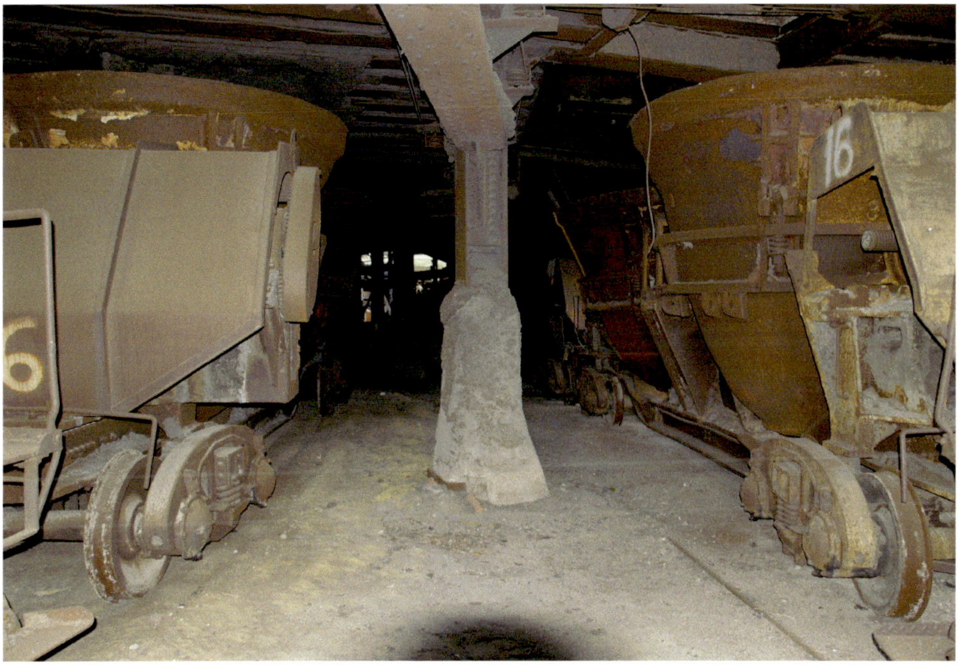

Railroad slag cars wait beneath a cast floor.

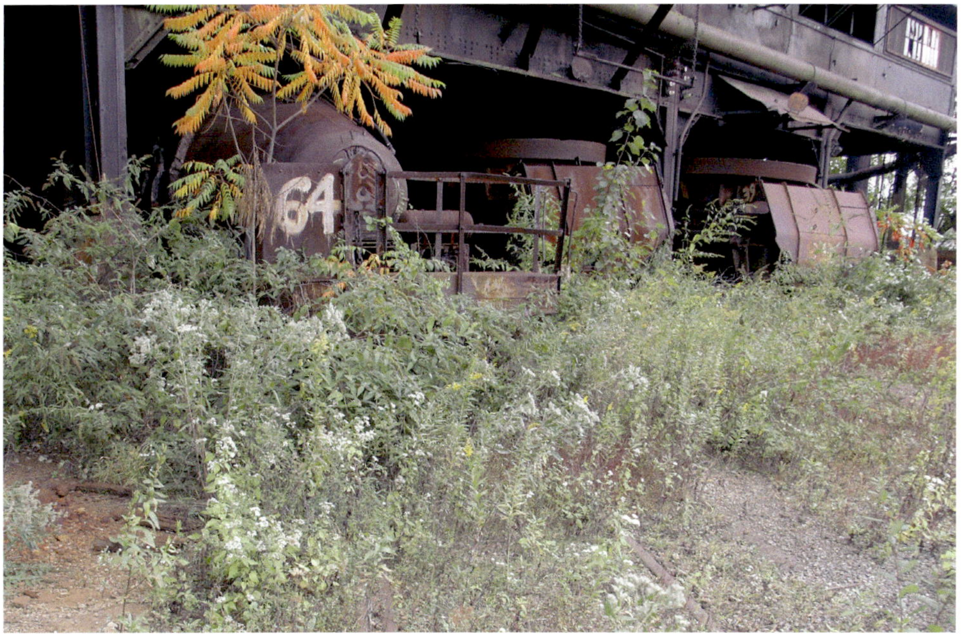

Nature has begun to reclaim the ground around a blast furnace. Hot metal Bottle Car #64 sticks out from under the cast floor, followed by two slag cars on separate railroad tracks to the right. The molten iron would be directed into bottle cars.

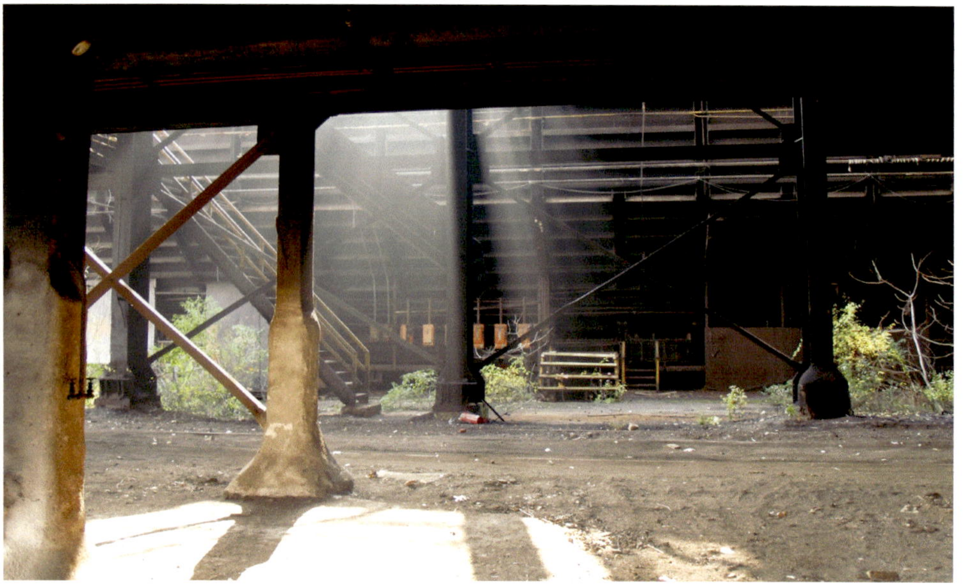

Morning light enters the area below the cast floor. Railroad tracks for slag/bottle cars can be faintly seen amid the layers of dirt and ash.

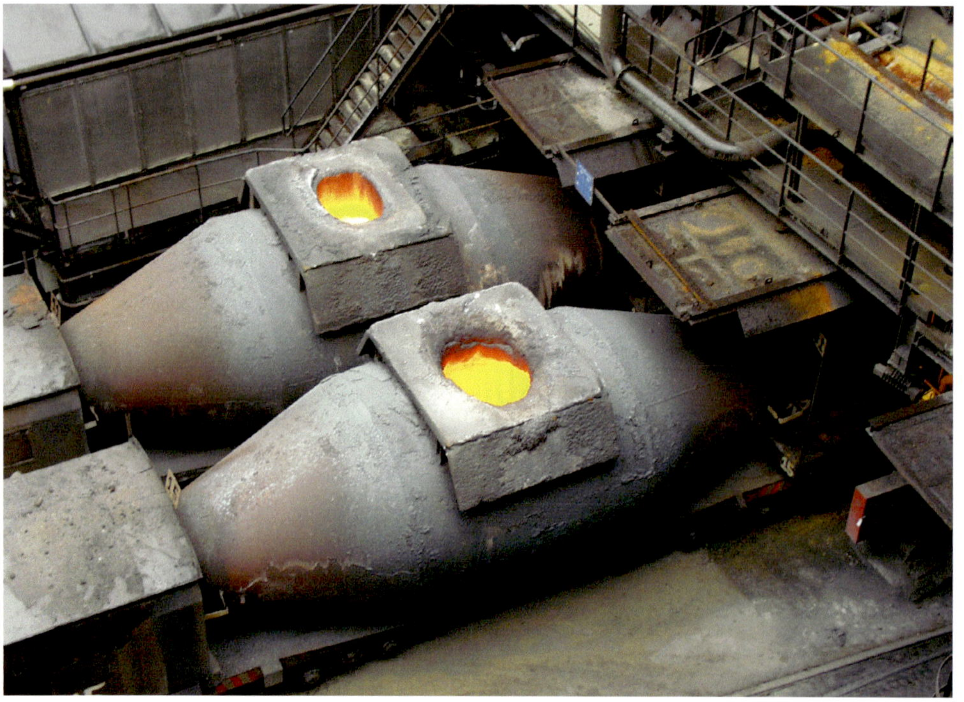

A bird's-eye view of hot metal railroad cars filled with molten metal at an unidentified steel plant. Their bottle shape is distinctly different from the teacup shape of slag cars. (*photograph credit: FreeImages.com*)

Forming steel to the customer's specifications was done by a variety of methods, often requiring reheating and rolling to make flat sheet steel, structural beams, seamless tubes, thin cable wire, rods, fasteners, and specialty products. Finally, the steel was fabricated and finish-shaped, machined, tempered (to harden), annealed (to make steel more workable), joined, tinned (to prevent rust), and finish-coated. During the fabrication and finishing processes, it was necessary to transfer partially completed products between the many separate, major buildings on Bethlehem Steel property, using some of the 400 miles of in-plant railroad track. Impressive as this sounds, the number of necessary movements on the way to the final product was painfully inefficient when contrasted with the relatively straight-line operations of competitive new steel plants that had been built away from crowded population centers, sometimes on virgin earth or even on the flattened ruins of war.

When Bethlehem Steel developed some new function for processing steel, a new building would also often be built. Then, railroad track would be laid to it, sometimes with switchbacks requiring locomotives to go forward and backward several times to position the railcar. The plant eventually grew to be nearly 4 miles long, yet only as wide as permitted by the narrow strip of land between Third Street of the city of Bethlehem and the Lehigh River.

Bethlehem Steel was considered an integrated steel mill, meaning they had the capabilities to perform every function of making steel, beginning with pretreatment of raw materials right through to finishing the product to the customer's specifications. Many steel companies worked on products that had some functions already done or that were yet to be done. Bethlehem Steel, and other integrated mills, were considered the purest form of steel mills.

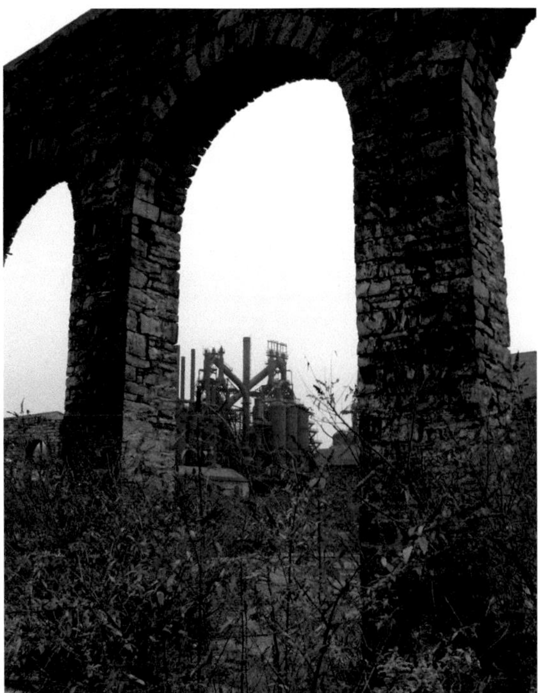

Blast Furnace A, Blast Furnace B, and the red roof of the Stock House reveal themselves from in between the carefully crafted stone archways of an abandoned and roofless building that formerly housed Bessemer converters and rolling mills.

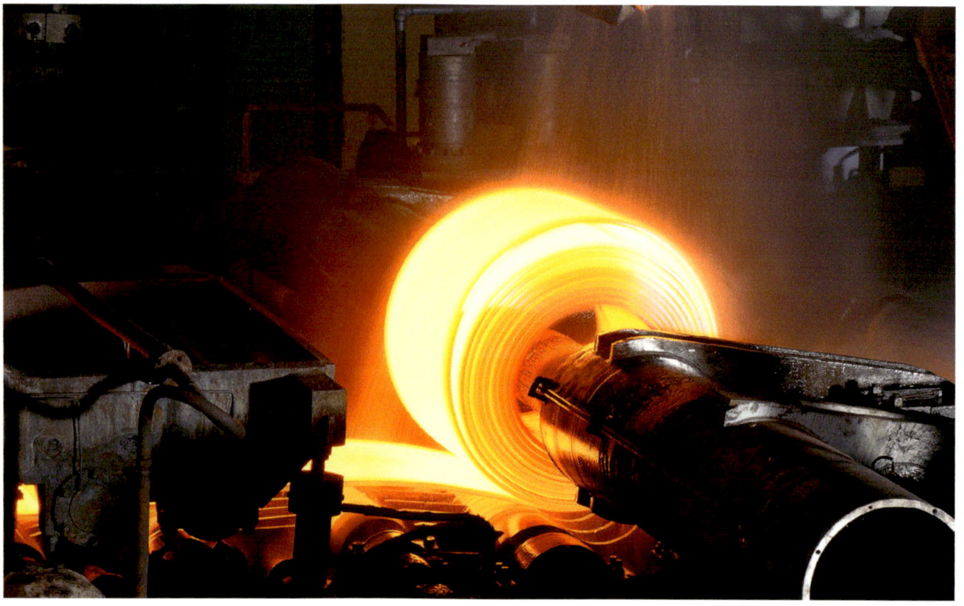

Hot rolling steel at an unidentified steel plant. (*photograph credit: Bigstock.com*)

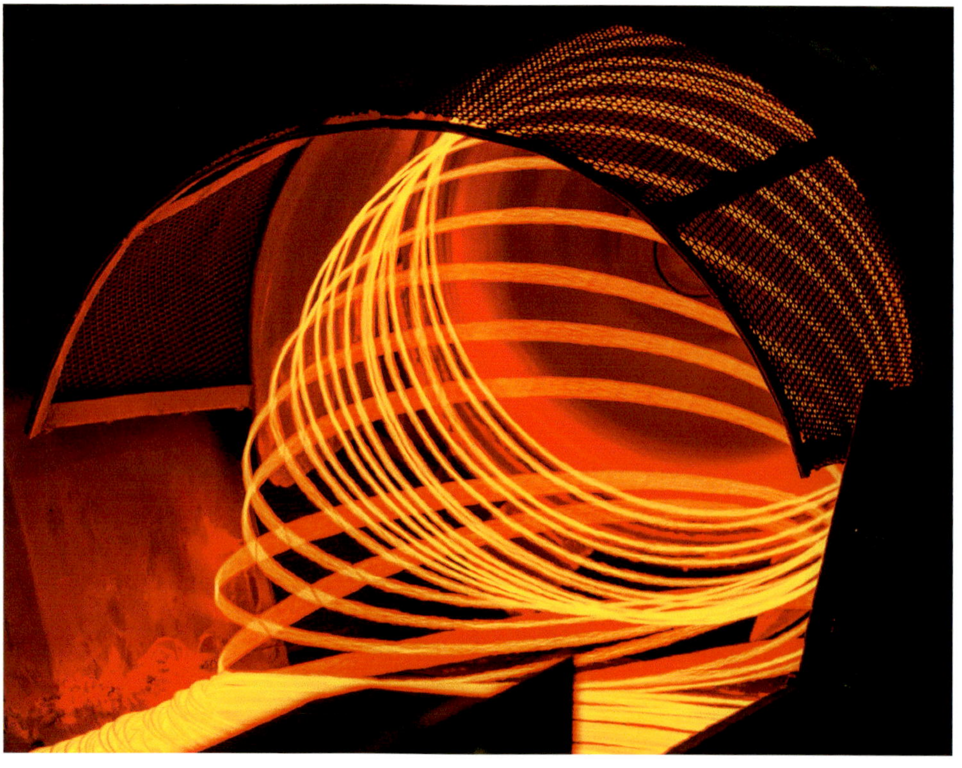

Manufacturing wire at an unidentified steel plant. (*photograph credit: Bigstock.com*)

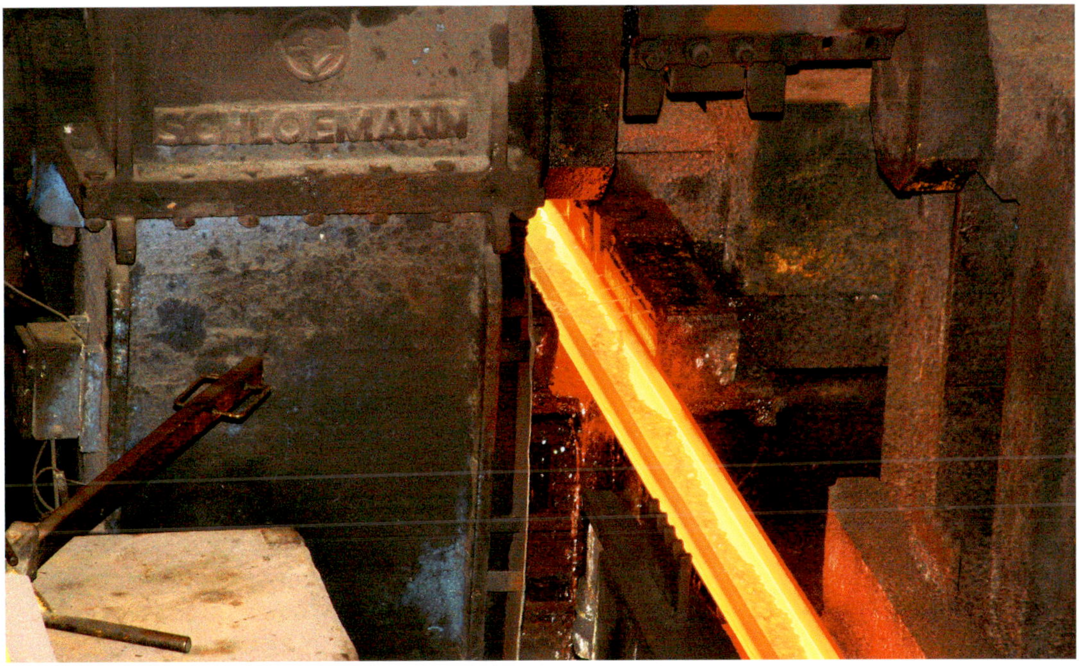

Rolling railway line at an unidentified steel plant. (*photograph credit: Bigstock.com*)

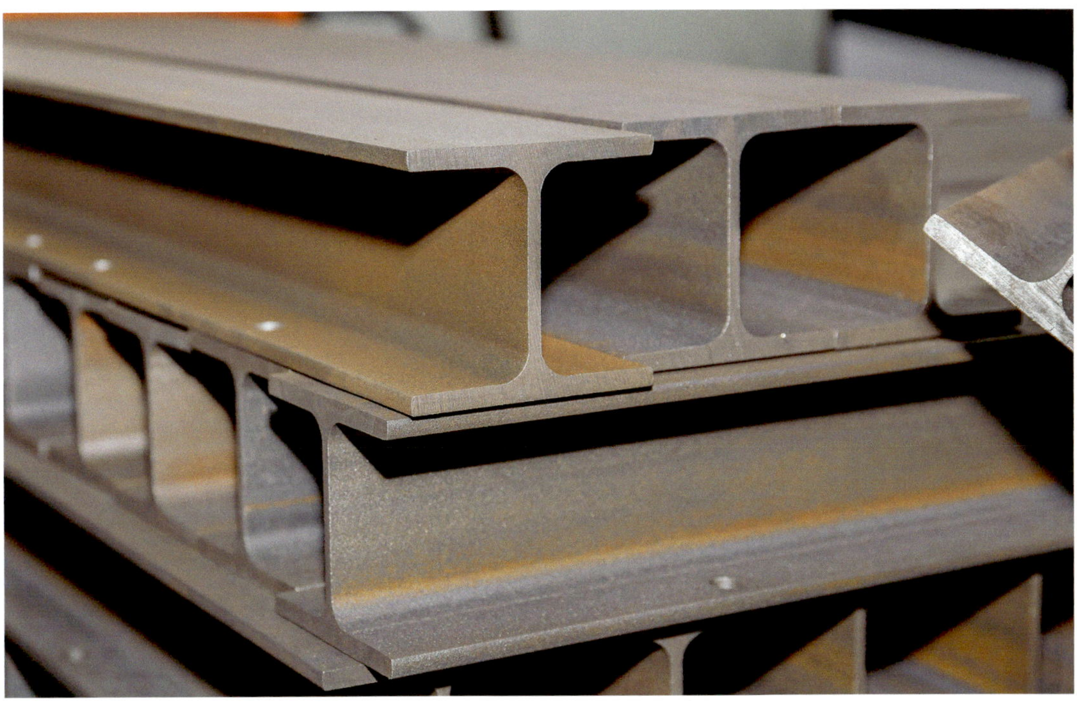

A stack of structural steel beams at an unidentified steel plant. (*photograph credit: Bigstock.com*)

8

INGENUITY AND INNOVATION

Necessity has resulted in some unique creations invented by the steel industry. Some are known everywhere steel is made and are still in use at steel mills around the world, but some were adopted by Bethlehem Steel with their own special twist on the concept, especially at their flagship Bethlehem plant. Here are a few examples, remnants of which are still visible.

Downcomers are heavy pipes coming down from the top of every furnace, named for their purpose of capturing excess hot gases from the iron smelting process, gases that would otherwise be sent into the atmosphere as waste.

At Bethlehem Steel, the downcomers from each furnace, up and down blast furnace row, were connected to a large-diameter pipe that carried the gases to one end of a long building, part of which still remains, called the Gas Blowing Engine House. In it, internal combustion engines were fueled by the excess gases to drive turbo blowers to make compressed air, with heavy flywheels using their momentum to steady the rotation of the engines' shafts. The compressed air was heated and blown into the furnaces to keep the smelting process consistent throughout the furnace as well as to make the fire hotter.

The other end of the long building, now gone, was the Lehigh Power House. Earlier in the last century, the power house produced electricity for the Bethlehem Steel plant. The carbon-rich gases captured by the downcomers were reburned by multiple engines with flywheels that connected to generators to make electricity.

The form of electricity that Bethlehem Steel made was classified as 25 Hz, commonly known as 25 cycle. It is technically a useful form of electricity to operate heavy electric motors in machines as well as the traction motors of larries, but lightbulbs in buildings tended to flicker with 25-cycle electricity, unlike the stability of 60-cycle standard household current. Nonetheless, generating their own electricity showed the innovation and self-sufficiency of Bethlehem Steel. They even sold electricity back to the local utility company.

Visible remains of the Gas Blowing Engine House can be seen from above when walking along the Hoover-Mason Trestle. There is also one of the 25-cycle generators and its large flywheel on the ground, left in its original position, even though the rest of the building that housed it has been demolished.

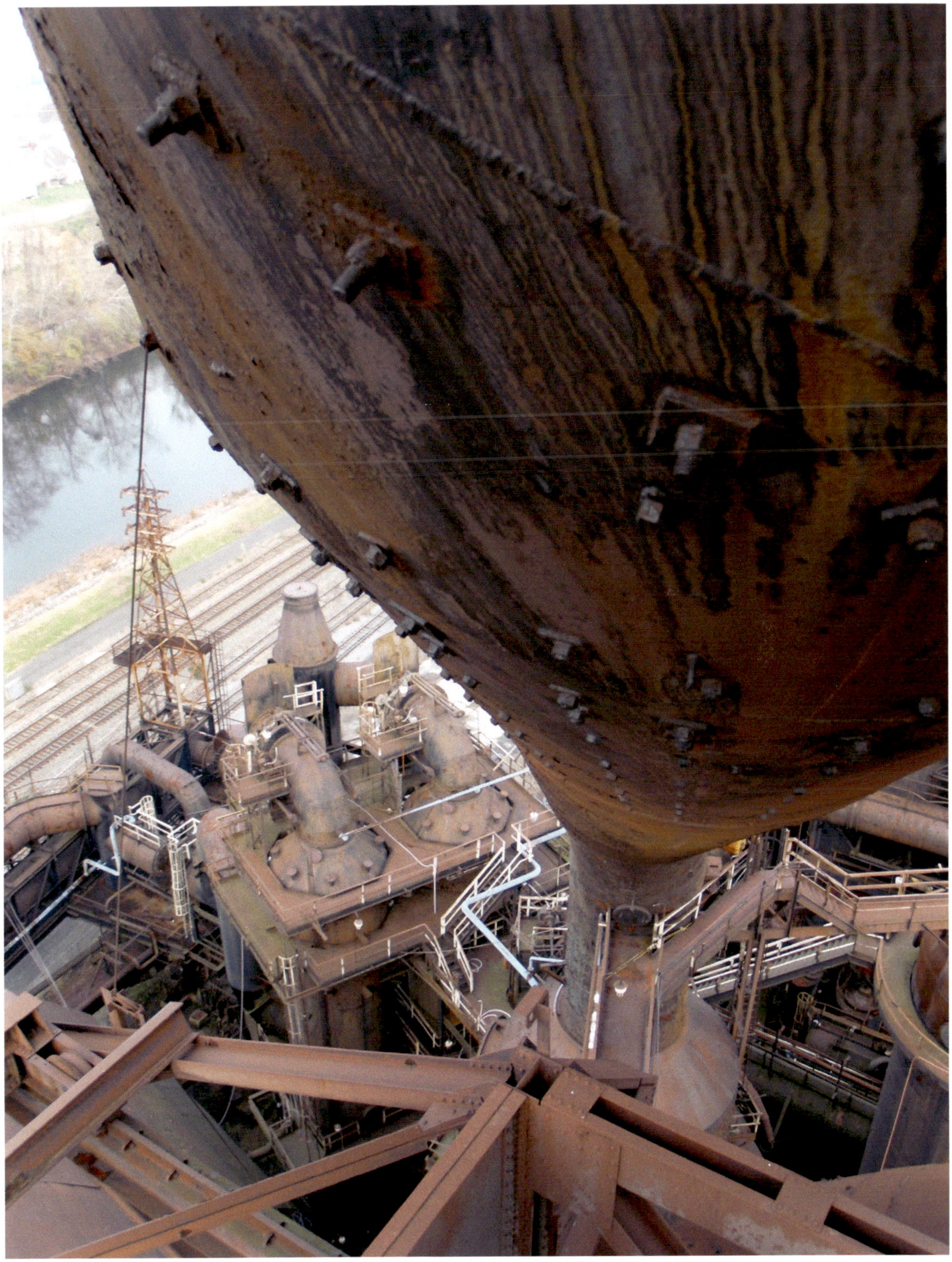

Looking at the underside of a downcomer pipe from the top of a blast furnace.

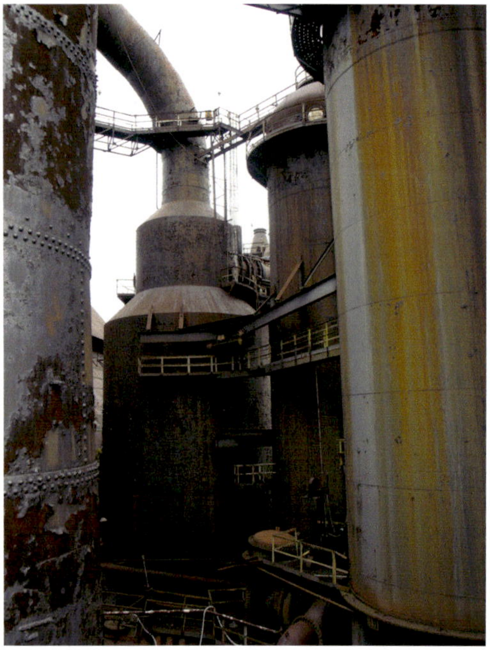

The downcomer pipe on its precipitous drop from the blast furnace would first filter hot waste air through a "dust catcher" (center) structure before it could be recycled. Stoves are also shown surrounding the dust catcher.

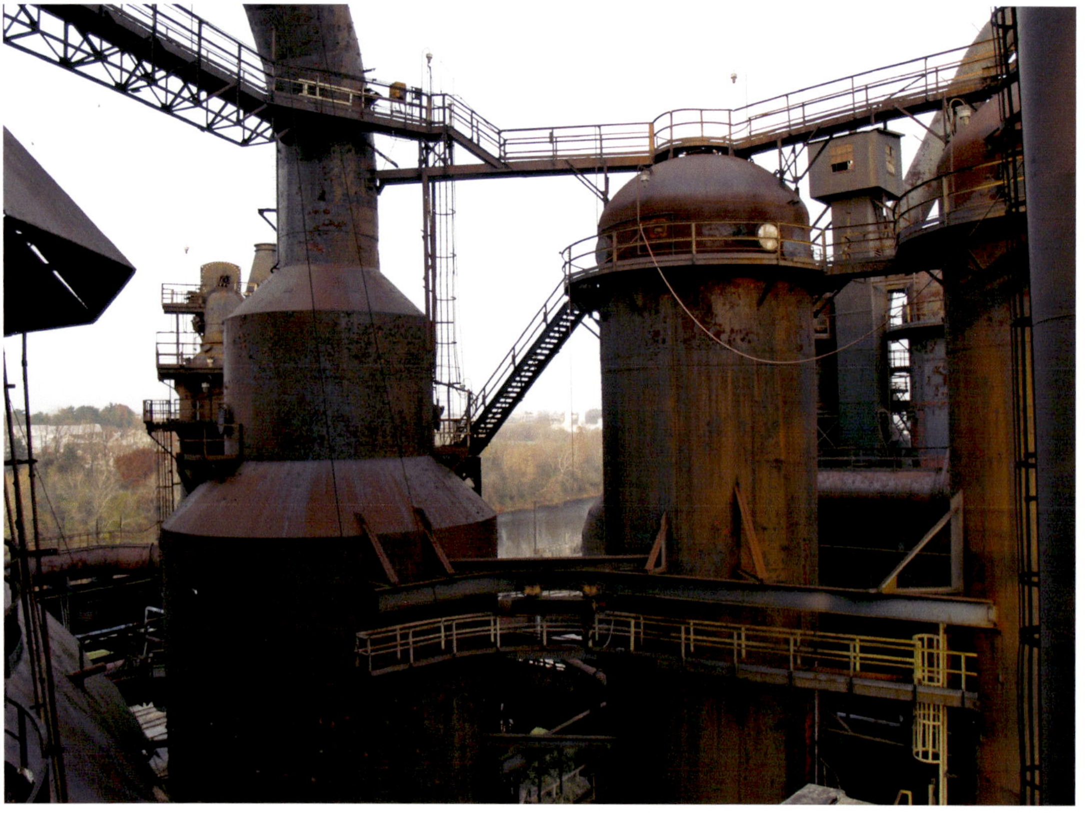

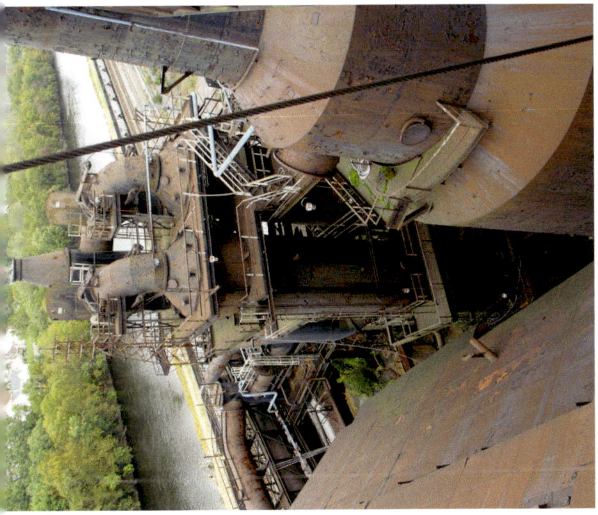

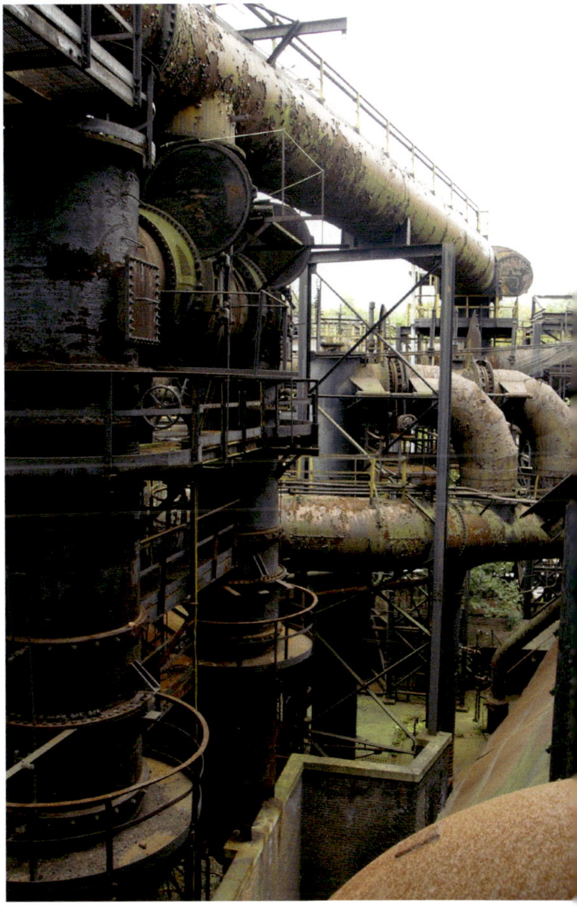

Above left: Additional gas cleaning equipment (center) followed the dust catcher (right) in the hot waste air recycling process.

Above right: A labyrinth of plumbing on a gigantic scale. Proper routing of air and gases was critical to the operation of the plant.

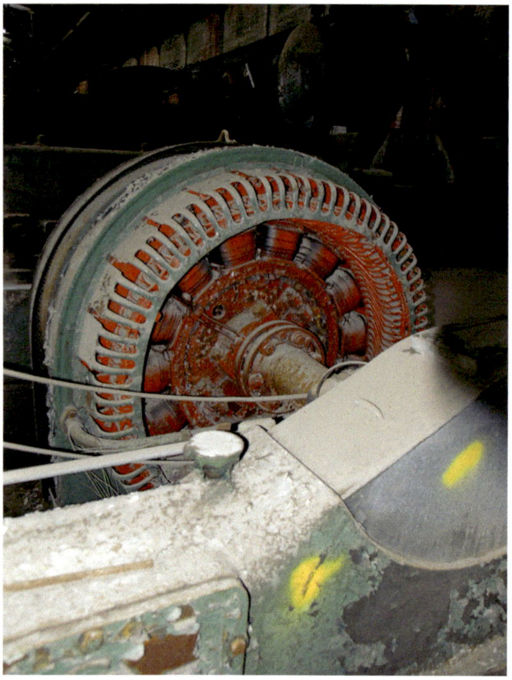

Left: Large vintage electric motor in the Gas Blowing Engine House/Lehigh Power House.

Below: Massive multi-ton flywheel in the Gas Blowing Engine House.

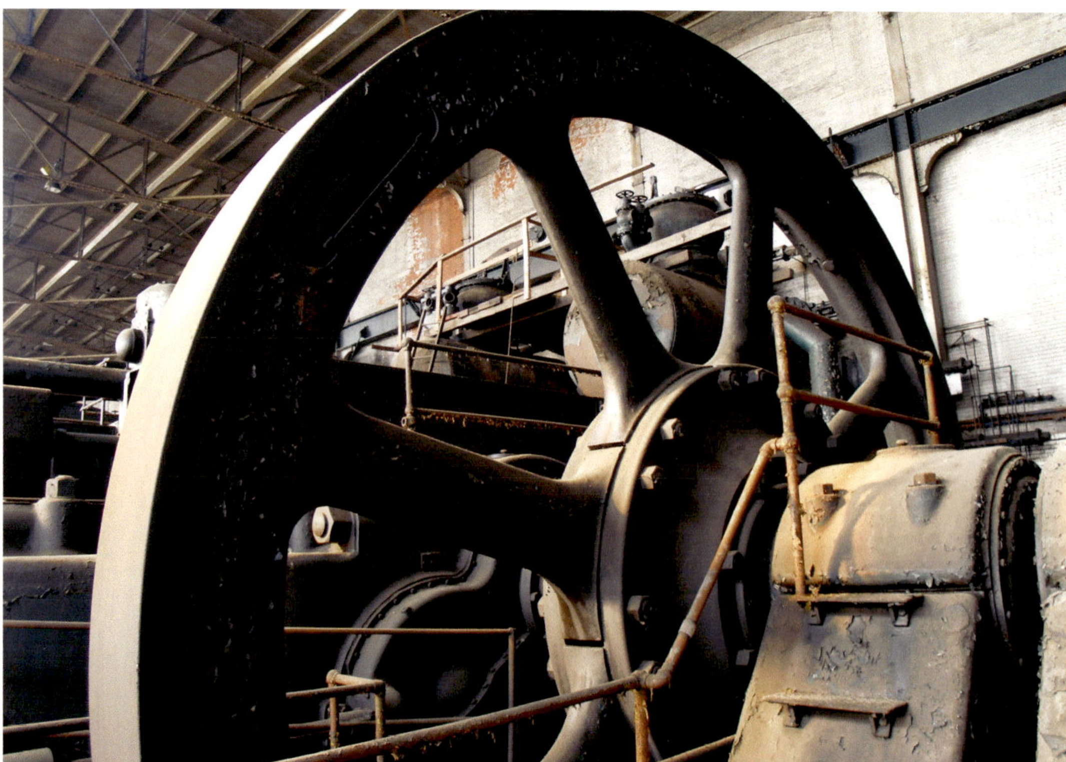

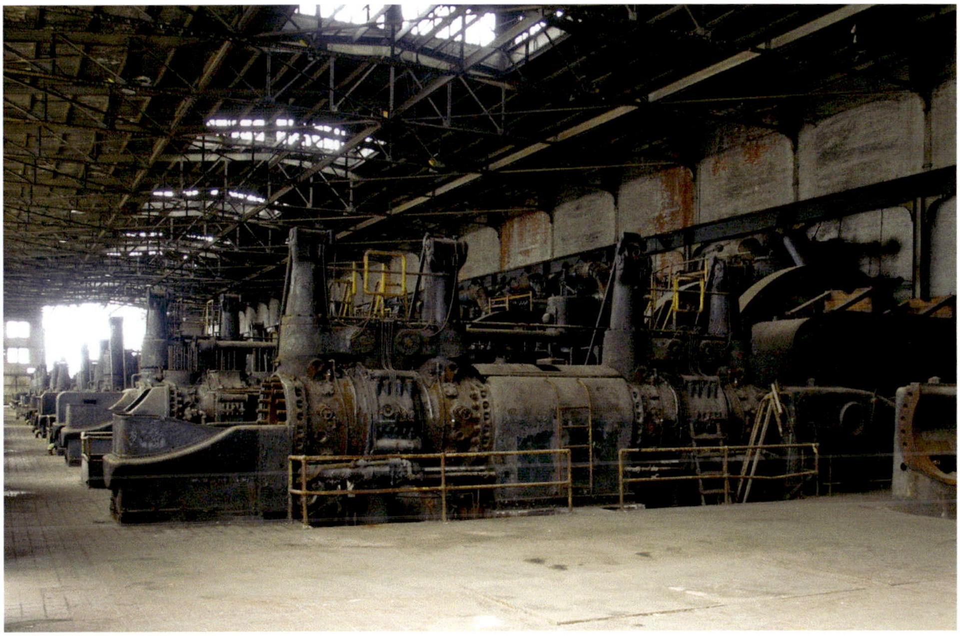

Inside the Gas Blowing Engine House.

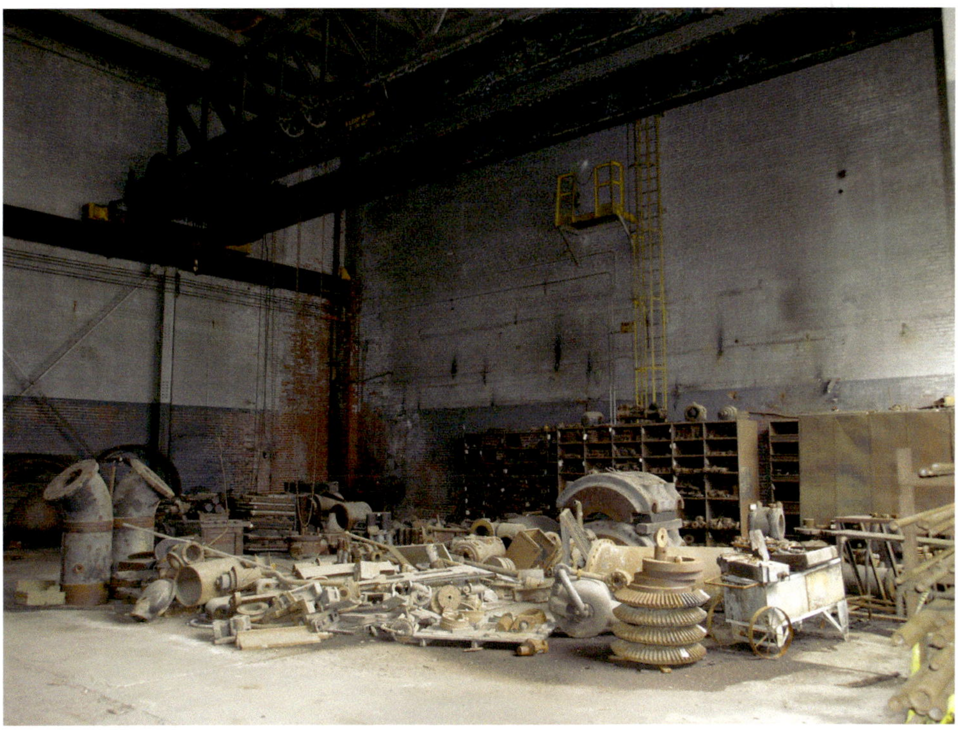

Parts for the gas-blowing engines.

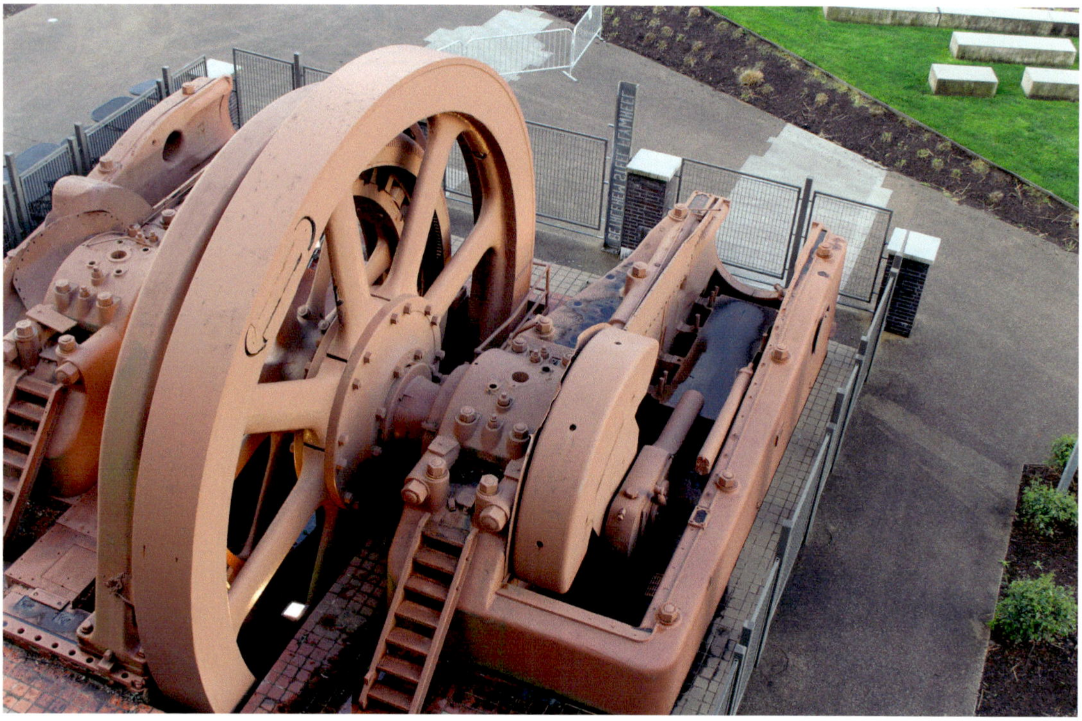

A remaining twenty-five-cycle generator that originally operated in the Lehigh Power House (demolished). Photograph taken in 2023.

The circular concrete base of a 30-foot-high water tower on the ground just beyond Furnace C is what remains of the Dorr plant, an innovative idea designed to reclaim waste as well as filter the air over the Bethlehem Steel site. The process began with an electrostatic accumulator, a tall pipe structure that produced static electricity. The atmosphere around a steel mill was always dusty with a content of microscopic metallic filings, invisible to the eye, but attracted by the static electricity. Once accumulated in a net, the dust was made into a thick, wet slurry, hence the need for the water tower, then dried and sintered, coalescing the loose particulate into a solid mass, much the way forming a hard snowball compresses loose snow together with hand pressure. The chunks or cakes of processed material were then fed back into the blast furnaces to add to the mixture making pig iron.

In the present day, cleaning the atmosphere around industrial plants is usually done with scrubbers, a variety of devices that remove particulates and gases from the air to reduce pollution. However, with the Dorr plant concept of the past, the steel industry was ahead of the curve in its concern for the quality of air near its facilities, with the tangible benefit to the company that a waste product, detrimental to air quality, was recycled back into the furnaces in a sort of continuous loop.

A giant railroad bumping post stands at the end of the Hoover-Mason Trestle, along with a red light that warns that it is the end of the trestle. The air brakes on a larry

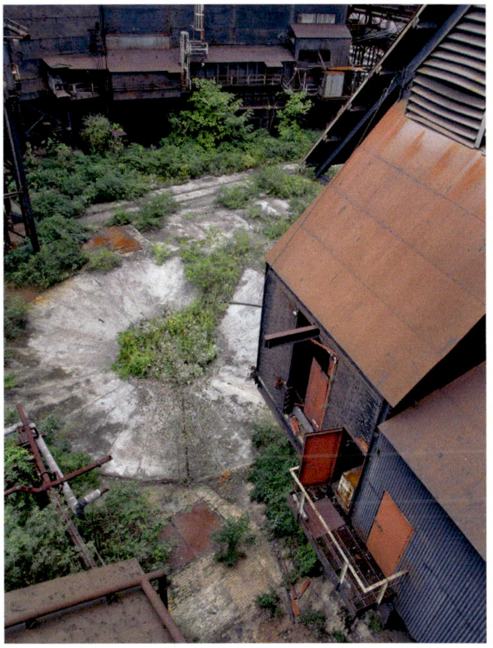

The circular foundations are all that remain of the former Dorr plant.

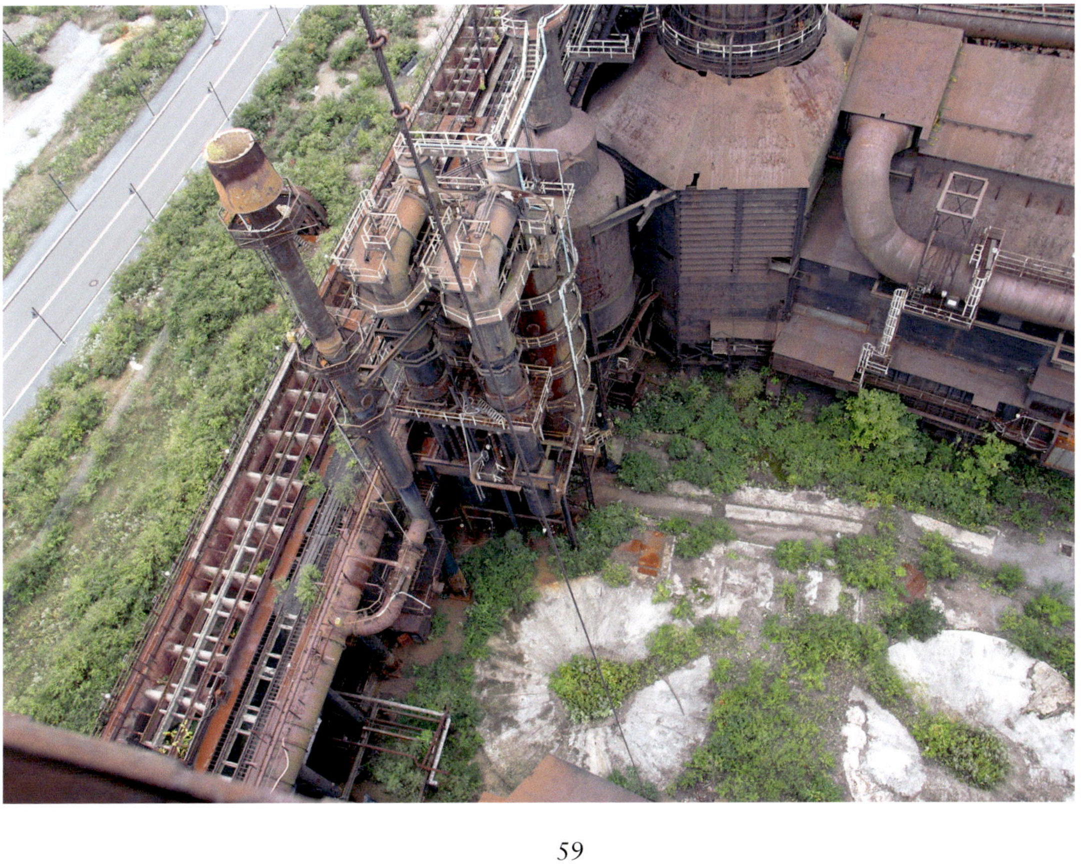

once failed, and the car went off the end of the 46-foot-high trestle and into the Stock House below.

Railroad bumping posts are often positioned at the end of a siding to keep cars from rolling off the end of the track, but the one that Bethlehem Steel had fabricated is heavy duty and exceptionally large. Its sections are designed to telescope into each other to absorb the force of a moving, 200-ton loaded ore car, should the occasion ever arise again.

When the new pedestrian walkway along the trestle was built, there was a proposal to use the larries to transport visitors and their tour guides past the blast furnaces. This has not happened yet, but if a larry is ever repurposed to carry tourists, the oversized bumping post may again be needed to stand guard and avoid an accident.

Workers who had to maintain or repair high parts of blast furnaces often had to climb steep open stairs or ladders while carrying heavy tools. A 1925 patent applied for by one Julian Kennedy of Pittsburgh, Pennsylvania, was entitled "elevator tower for blast furnace structures" and showed engineering drawings of a cylindrical elevator to access the heights of blast furnaces. The elevator's tubular form did not require external bracing because its structure was comprised of several jointed rings or bands that gave strength and even prevented water and gas from getting in. At the top, the elevator was connected to the blast furnace with a "bracing connection" including a platform and a "motor room."

Julian Kennedy received his patent in 1927, and cylindrical elevators began being built at steel mills. On the Bethlehem Steel site, the elevators first appear to be smokestacks, but their red doors reveal they are instead Kennedy's patented elevators that could safely carry a worker at least partway to the heights.

The obvious importance of the steel industry to America encouraged creative minds to come up with innovative ideas that made the activities of a steel mill more productive, safer for workers, and sometimes even more friendly to the communities in which they were located.

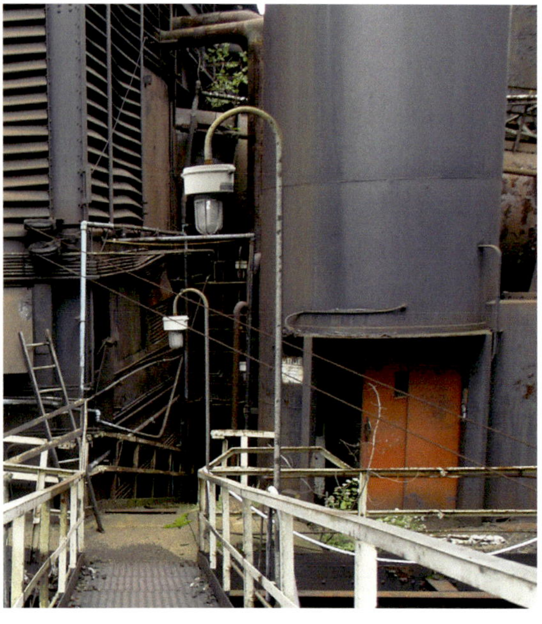

The base of a cylindrical elevator with its characteristic sliding red door.

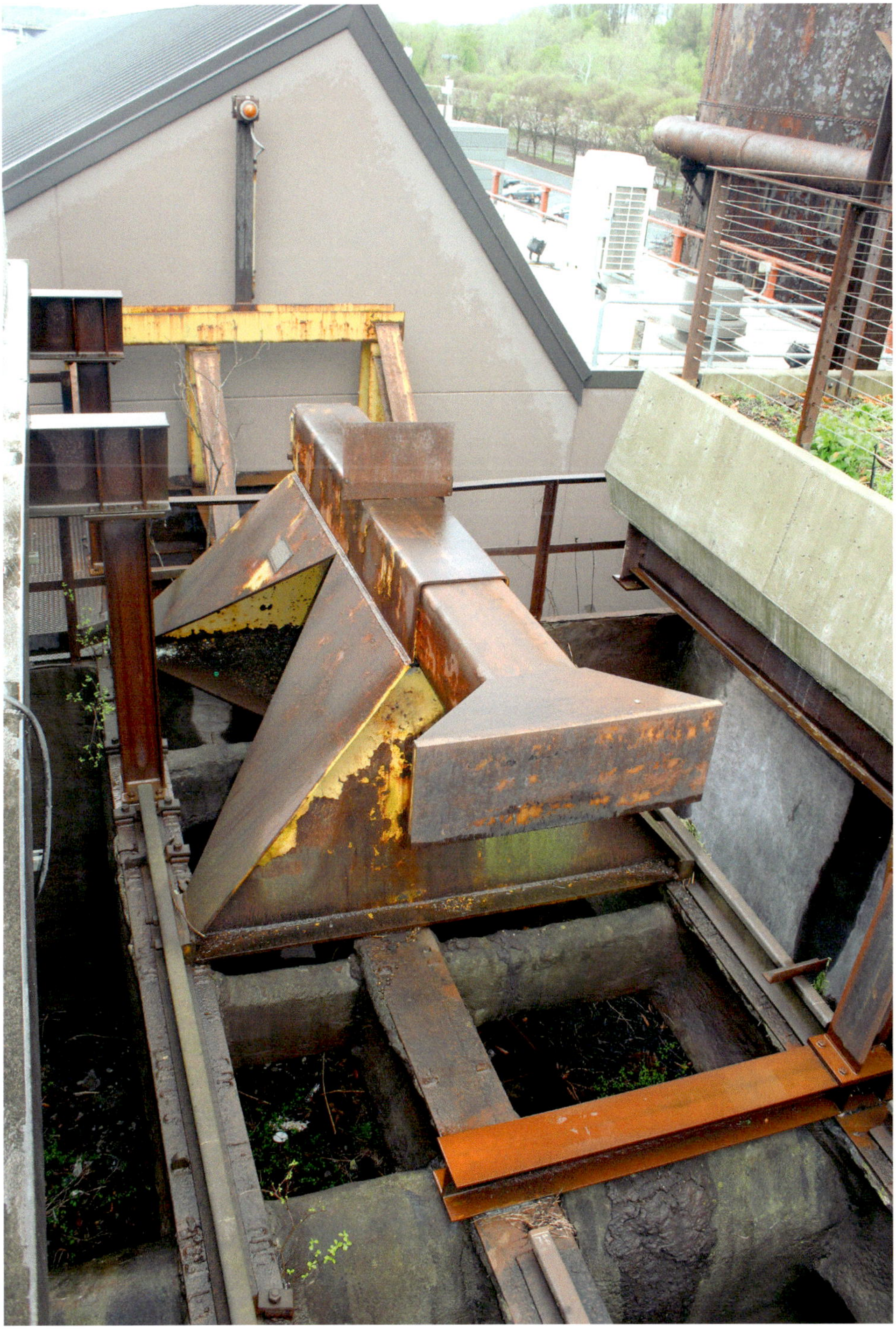

Heavy-duty railroad bumping post with red light signifying the end of the trestle. The restored Stock House roof appears in the background. Photograph taken in 2023.

9

WORKING AT BETHLEHEM STEEL: MANAGEMENT

The top executives of Bethlehem Steel enjoyed the challenge of making more and more profits for stockholders and for themselves. They lived well on the job ... and at home.

Senior management worked in the Bethlehem Steel General Office, a 1916 brick building designed in an "H" shape that permitted as many corner offices as possible. The elegant marble lobby of the office building was adorned with a daily bouquet of cut flowers to greet customers. Carefully chosen women were receptionists, secretaries, elevator operators, and guides who led customers to the offices on upper floors. The Carpentry and Pattern Shop, in close proximity to the corporate offices, made the fine furniture for executives' offices. The General Office building was originally seven floors, but six more floors were later added, prompting superstitious employees to question the wisdom of a thirteen-story building.

In the late 1950s, nine of the twelve top wage earners in the United States worked for Bethlehem Steel. In 1956, CEO Eugene Grace was the highest-paid executive in the country. In 1959, it was Bethlehem Steel's president, Arthur Homer, who commanded the highest salary in all of American industry, in excess of $500,000 (in 1950s currency), plus bonuses. Also making high salaries were eight levels of middle managers between the president of the company and the workers on the factory floor.

Whenever a new union contract increased workers' wages, management took the opportunity to raise their own salaries. An additional luxury that management afforded themselves was building a golf course anywhere they built a new plant.

In 1972, the corporate offices were moved to Martin Tower, a $35 million steel high-rise building several miles north of the plant. Top management now had a view from the tallest building in the Lehigh Valley. A cross-shaped architectural configuration once again permitted additional corner offices. After Bethlehem Steel no longer existed, it was hoped Martin Tower could be saved by leasing offices to Union Pacific Railroad, Dun & Bradstreet, and others. Repurposing the building as condos also seemed a possibility to give it new life, but the expense of a sprinkler system and asbestos removal was the death knell for the building, and it was demolished by implosion in May 2019.

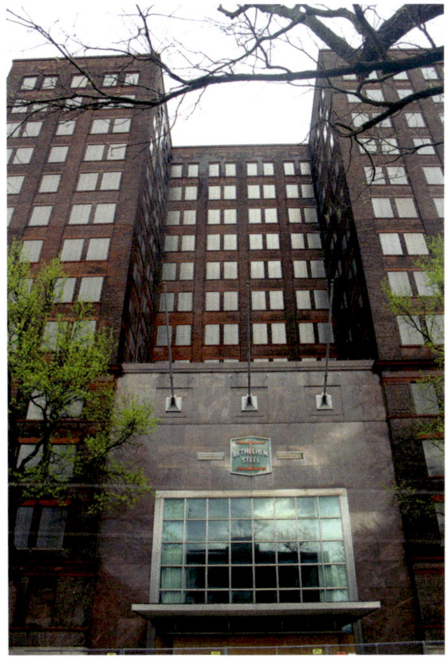

Right: The "H" shape of the 1916 General Office is readily apparent. Photograph taken in 2023.

Below: Paying tribute to the famous 1935 photograph by Walker Evans, this 2006 scene from St. Michael's Cemetery additionally portrays Martin Tower (far upper left) before it was demolished.

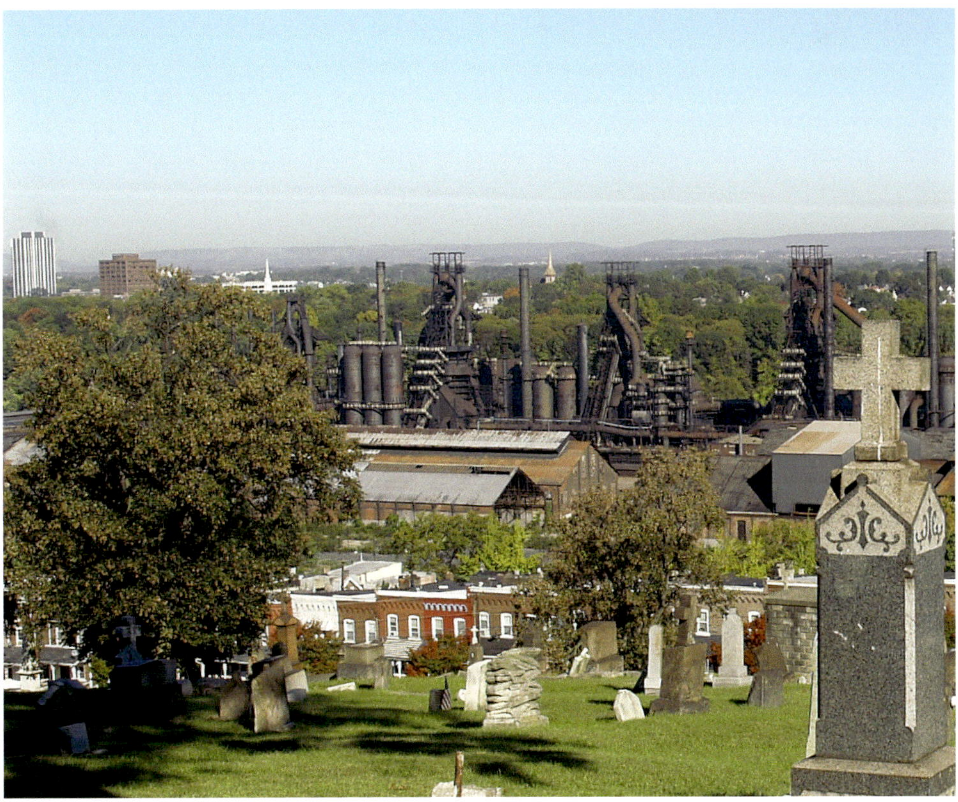

10

WORKING AT BETHLEHEM STEEL: LABOR

For workers on the floor, especially in the early days, danger constantly lurked. It was hard work, usually noisy, always hot and dirty. Some reports indicated that in 1909, 10 percent of the workers in labor jobs died in industrial accidents, and 21 percent were injured in the dangerous working conditions. In those days, long before OSHA (Occupational Safety and Health Administration) guidelines, sometimes a long-sleeve flannel shirt was the main article of clothing to protect arms from sparks and bits of flying metal. The work was physically challenging, and there were always complaints, but it provided a decent salary.

It was common for the generation working at Bethlehem Steel to have a father and even a grandfather who had worked at the plant, and the upcoming younger generation also expected to find good employment at The Steel. Workers had a real sense of pride in knowing they were literally building America.

More than thirty different nationalities were represented in hard-hat jobs at Bethlehem Steel. German and Hungarian were among the earliest. Many continued to speak their native languages, but workers of varying countries and ethnic backgrounds found ways to communicate and get along with each other in a healthy competition. The Polish guy did not want the Irish guy to look like he was doing a better job, but more importantly, workers watched out for each other. Everyone wanted to go home safely from a shift.

Adding to the diversity of workers at The Steel were women, not only in the offices, but in labor jobs. During World War II, when 30,000 employees worked at the flagship Bethlehem plant, 2,200 women replaced men fighting overseas. At first, male employees resented women on the floor, but seeing the excellent job they did, the men gradually accepted women in hard-hat jobs. When the war ended, the women were sent back home, but legal action in the 1970s forced the company to again hire women in labor jobs.

Among the most respected and highly skilled jobs at the plant were the riggers, the workers who could fix anything. They immediately responded to the need to repair something because the plant had to operate 24/7, 365 days, no matter the season,

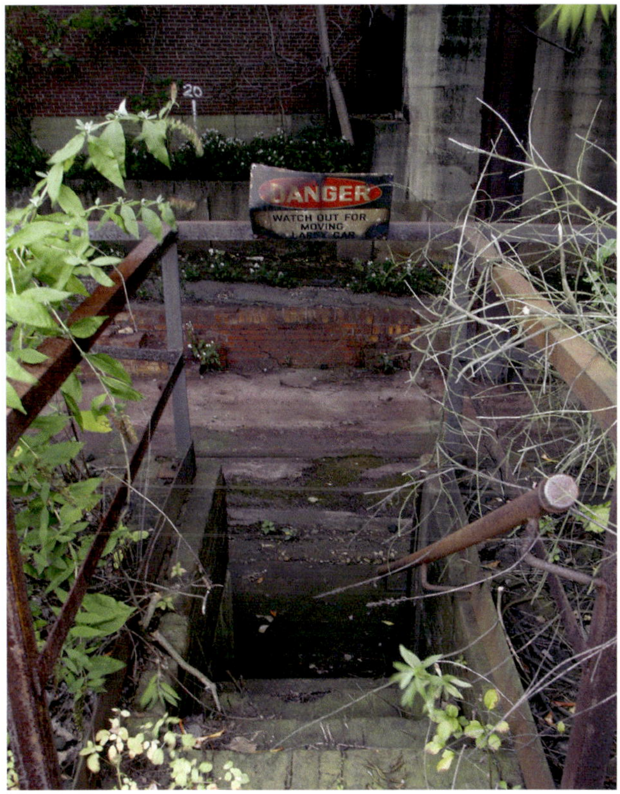

Danger warning signs were ubiquitous throughout the Bethlehem Steel plant.

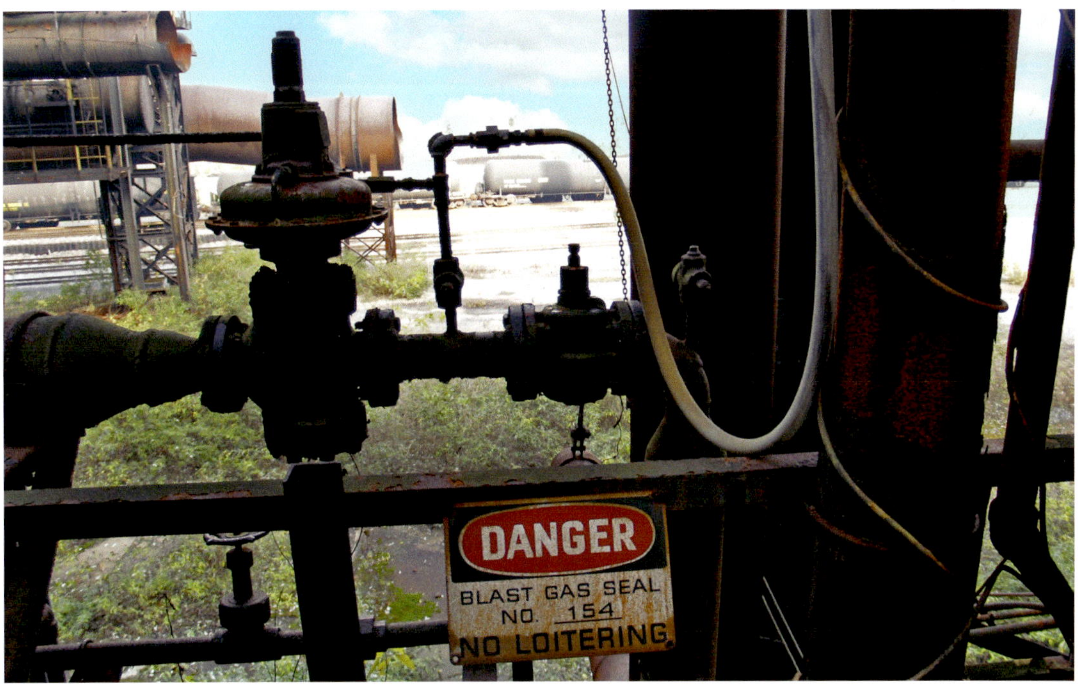

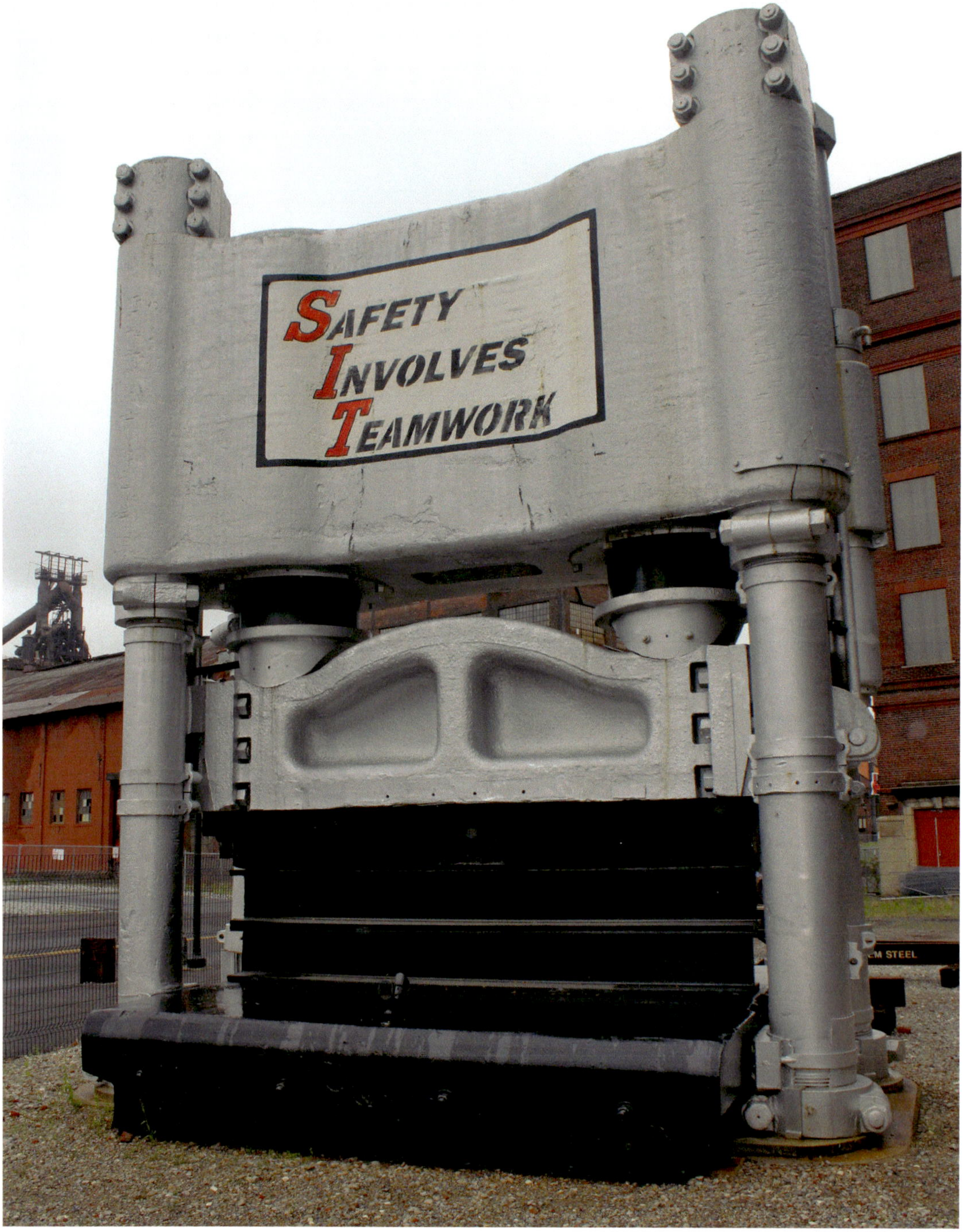

A vintage bending press wears the slogan: "Safety Involves Teamwork." This press was first put into service around 1890 and was actively used for over a century. It served a number of purposes including shaping armor plate for battleships. Photograph taken in 2023.

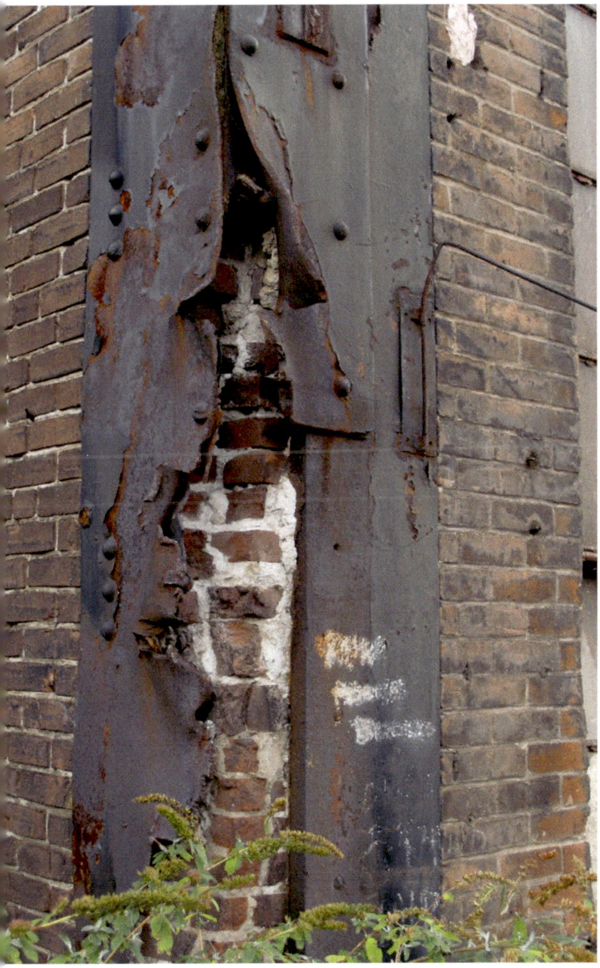

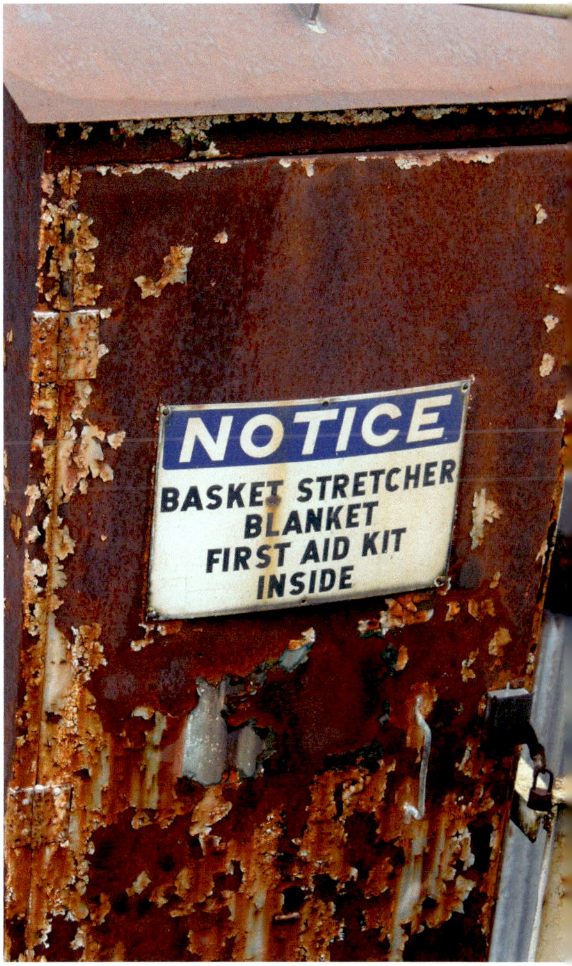

Above left: Whatever accidentally collided with this wall managed to tear through riveted steel corner bracing.

Above right: An emergency aid station along the Hoover-Mason Trestle. Photograph taken in 2023.

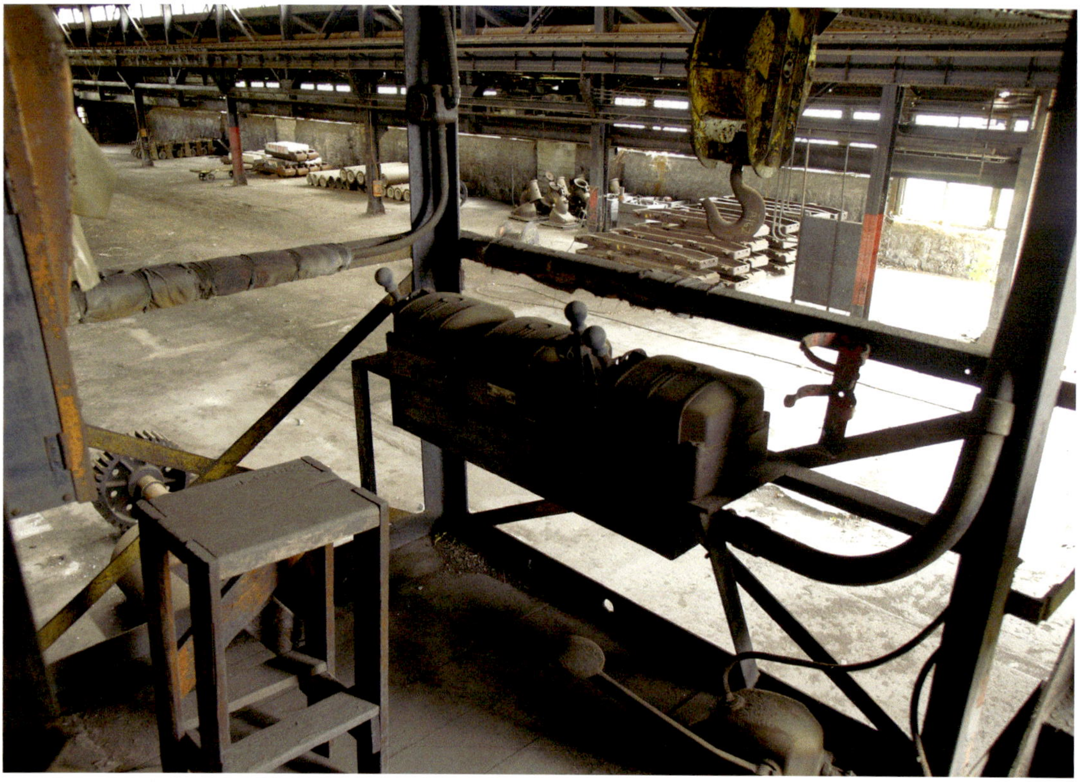

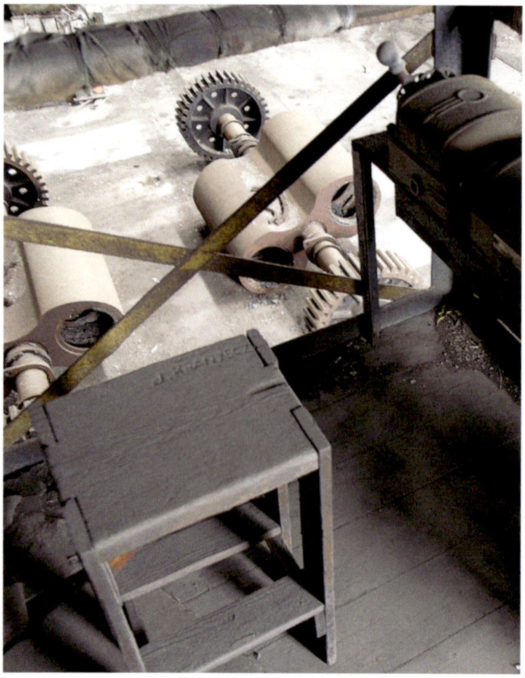

Above: View from the hoist operator's bench in the Turn & Grind Shop.

Left: Note the hoist operator's name proudly carved into the wooden bench.

weather, or time of day or night. Riggers were risk-takers. Much of the time they worked on the ground, but if something became inoperative high up, they generally had to fix it without the chance to erect scaffolding or the benefit of a safety net.

The age and experience of workers varied widely. Older workers willingly taught younger workers, but there were exceptions. Sometimes an older worker feared that the newbie might someday take their job, so occasionally there was a hesitancy to explain all aspects and nuances of a specialized task.

To improve working conditions for labor, management was pressured to permit "welfare rooms" at various locations around the plant. These were places where workers could change their clothes before and after a shift. A unique basket system permitted street clothes and other belongings to be hoisted up high and locked for security during a shift.

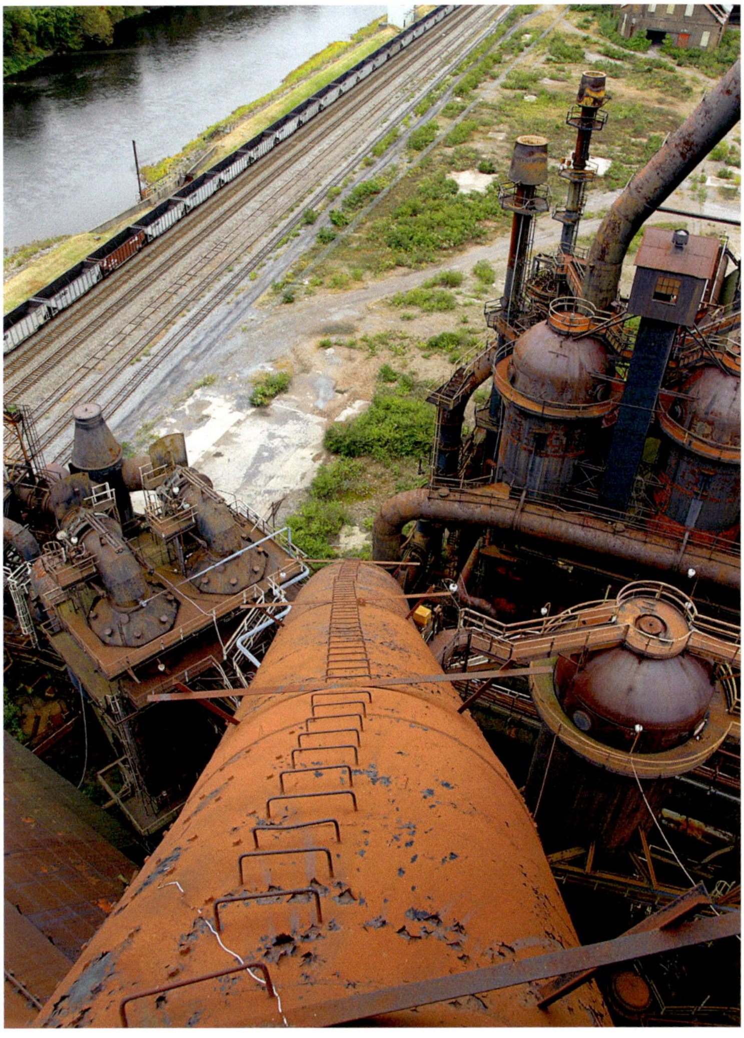

Riggers needed to be comfortable with climbing and with fall exposure. This is looking down a massive downcomer pipe from the top of Blast Furnace D. In the distance, railroad hopper cars (often seen loaded with coal or coke) simply pass by this silenced steel plant on their way to a different destination.

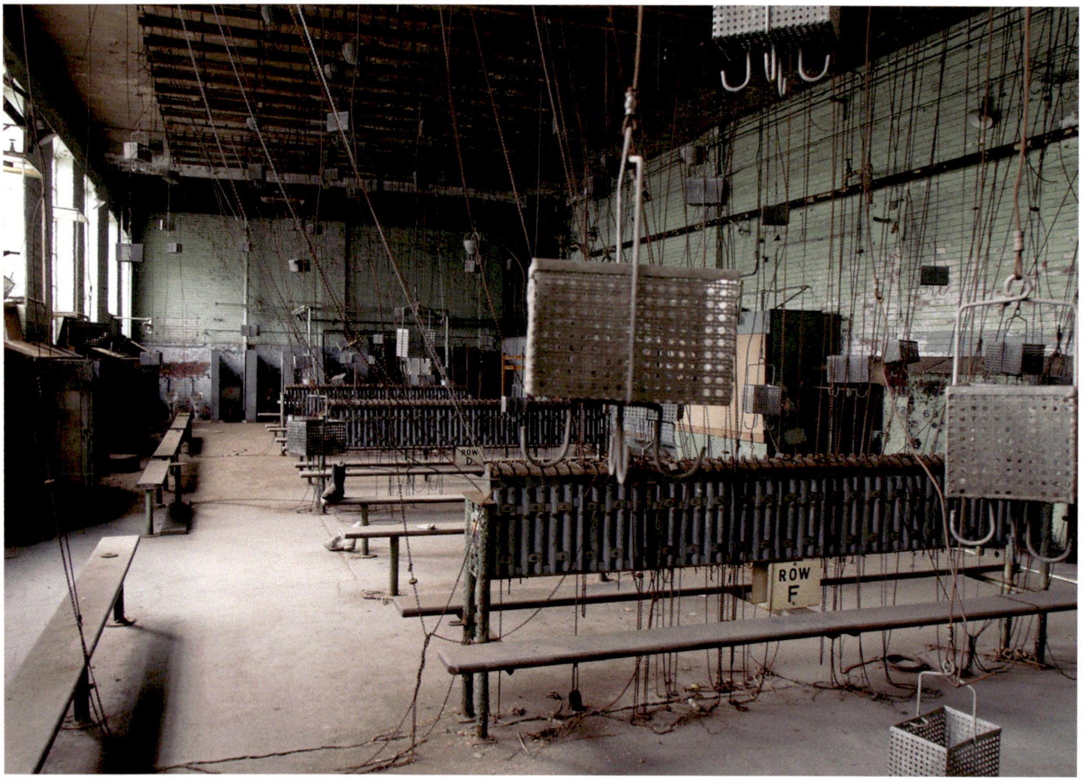

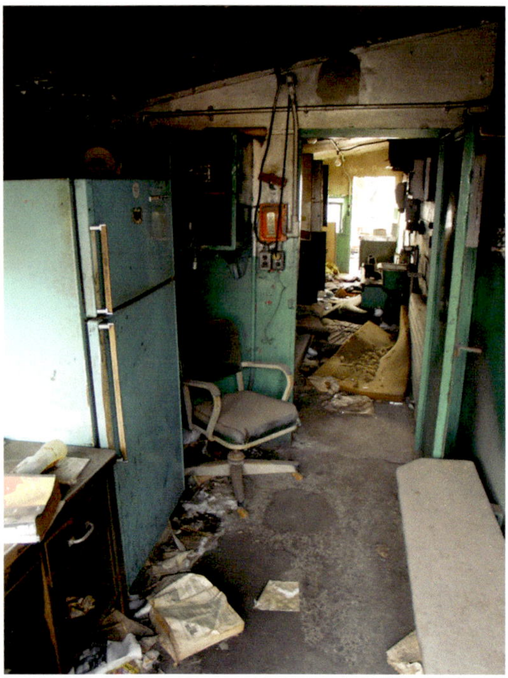

Above: One of the welfare rooms at Bethlehem Steel. The raised baskets held a worker's personal effects safely out of reach from others. Near the center/left of the photograph, a pair of abandoned boots awaits their owner's return.

Left: A former break room near the blast furnaces.

11

THE LABOR UNION MOVEMENT

Dissatisfaction with some aspect of their employment caused labor to stage several major work stoppages over the years. A bitter 1910 strike was over low wages and the resulting need to work overtime, often already forced by management, to make enough money to survive. When tempers flared, company owner Charles M. Schwab called in mounted Pennsylvania State Police who charged into the crowd with billy clubs, injuring some of the strikers and making them even angrier. After 108 days, most workers went back on the job with no satisfactory settlement having been reached.

Workers' wanting to be represented by a national labor union caused another job action that began in March 1941. The Steel Workers' Organizing Committee staged a work stoppage that only lasted four days, but the strike once again turned violent when cars owned by strikebreakers and company executives were overturned and burned. Pressured by awareness that the United States would again be called into an expanding European war, management reluctantly permitted collective bargaining with the United Steelworkers of America, a strong union that replaced management's own weak representation plan for labor, which lacked any ability to strike.

The strength of the union was clearly shown in 1959, when a 117-day nationwide steel strike virtually crippled the country, ultimately affecting every aspect of American life. The strike was largely over management's demands for renegotiating union contracts because the efficiency of new machines required fewer operators. Citing a national emergency caused by the strike, President Dwight D. Eisenhower invoked a clause of the Taft-Hartley Act for the first time. It forced workers back on the job during negotiations. Vice President Richard Nixon led talks between labor and management to end the strike, resulting in major wage increases and improved employee pension and health care benefits.

In the second half of the twentieth century, technological progress in steelmaking reduced labor costs, but cumbersome work rules demanded by United Steelworkers of America diluted any financial advantages the company could accrue. In addition, workers' wages far outpaced the price the company could get for a ton of steel.

12

DECLINE AND DEMISE

Bethlehem Steel's long downhill slide was brought on by numerous factors, some of which were not able to be controlled by the company, while others required more attention and financial investment than was given.

Bethlehem Steel was coming off huge profits from World War II and the post-war building boom, and it seemingly bolstered the company's erroneous belief that this would continue forever. It was unfortunate that management appeared to lack effective foresight to see beyond the good times. Aluminum, pre-stressed structural concrete, plastics, and new synthetic materials were reducing the worldwide demand for steel, adversely affecting the entire industry.

In addition, traditional old ways of making steel were clearly giving way to the new, and the company lacked the agility to effectively respond. In the decades after World War II, mini mills in various areas of the United States, including the Deep South, as well as Europe and Asia, started making steel with the electric arc furnace (EAF) method, an extremely hot furnace that was fed scrap steel—everything from automobiles to home appliances—and out came new steel. In the process, graphite electrodes conduct electric current into the furnace. Mini mills simplified the steelmaking process, bypassing first making pig iron in a blast furnace. With new production methods, what used to take ten man-hours to make 1 ton of steel now took just one-half man-hour.

In the 1960s and 1970s, Bethlehem Steel management sunk $7.2 billion into more fully embracing modern production methods, including some electric arc furnaces, and even built a new plant. However, in a tumultuous rollercoaster ride, years of record sales were often followed by record losses, and periods of unprecedented production were followed by capacity reduction to conserve cash. Any positive action Bethlehem Steel took to avoid a downhill slide appeared to be too little and too late.

In the early 1960s, the price of steel worldwide was at all-time lows, and competition from imported steel had been greatly harming sales across the entire industry. In addition, the image of "big steel" was tarnished in 1962 when steel companies nationwide raised the price of steel 3½ percent across the board, just as the United States was struggling to end a recession. Back then, President John F. Kennedy framed it as a class struggle

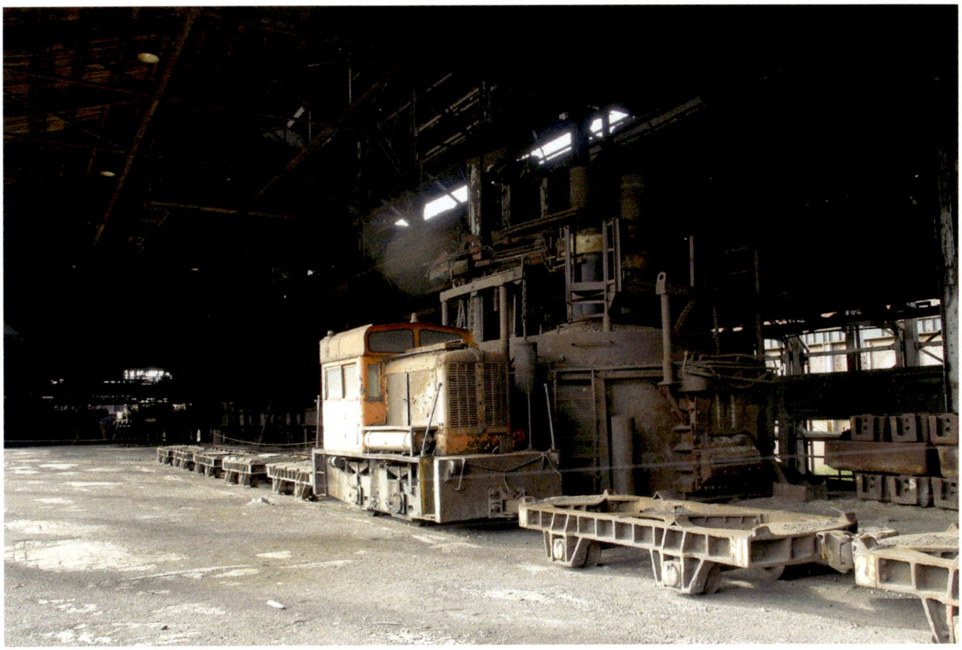

Diesel-electric-powered locomotive switcher and four-wheel "charging buggies" in front of an electric arc furnace (EAF) in the former Electric Furnace Melt Shop. This locomotive has now been restored and occasionally operates for tourists in front of the National Museum of Industrial History (formerly Bethlehem Steel's Electric Repair Shop).

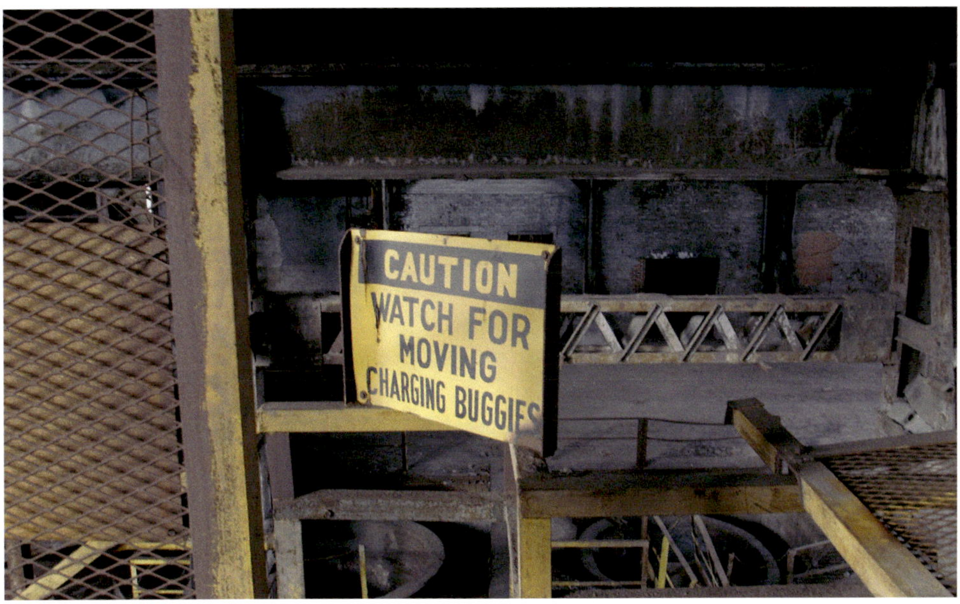

Caution sign warning workers to watch for moving charging buggies. Charging buggies carried scrap metal and other material to the electric arc furnaces.

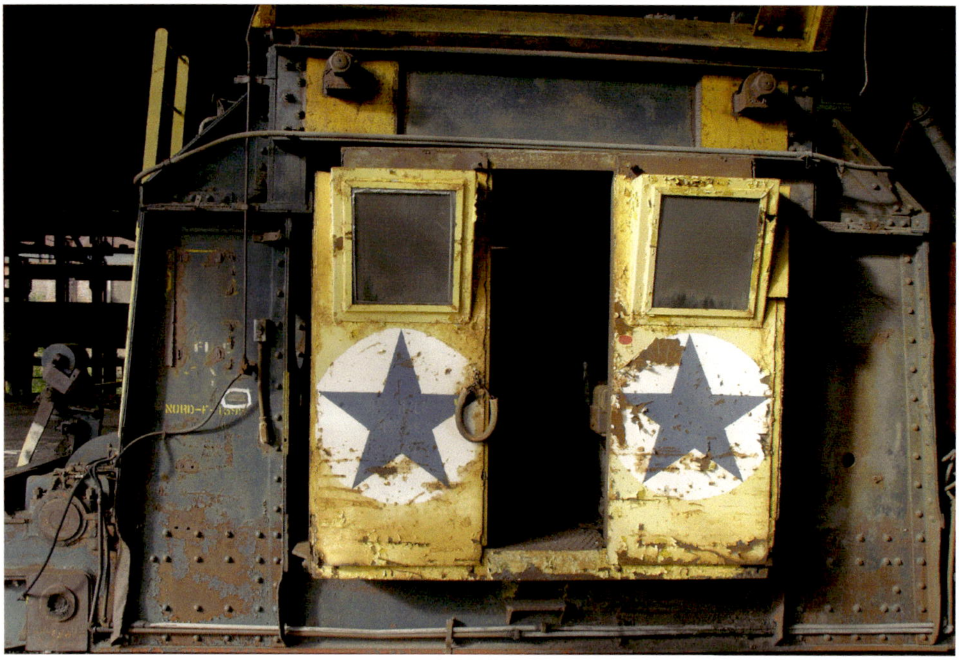

A charging machine that operated on rails alongside the charging buggies. With a long rotating arm (out of view), it carried scrap metal from the charging buggies and loaded it into the electric arc furnaces. This charging machine has since been repainted and preserved in front of the National Museum of Industrial History.

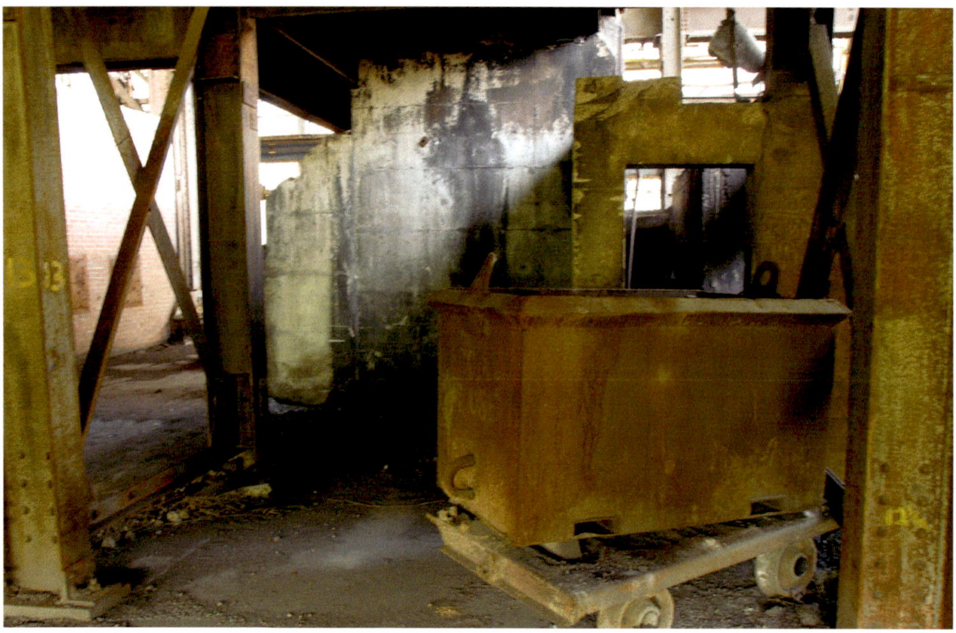

A scene from the Electric Furnace Melt Shop.

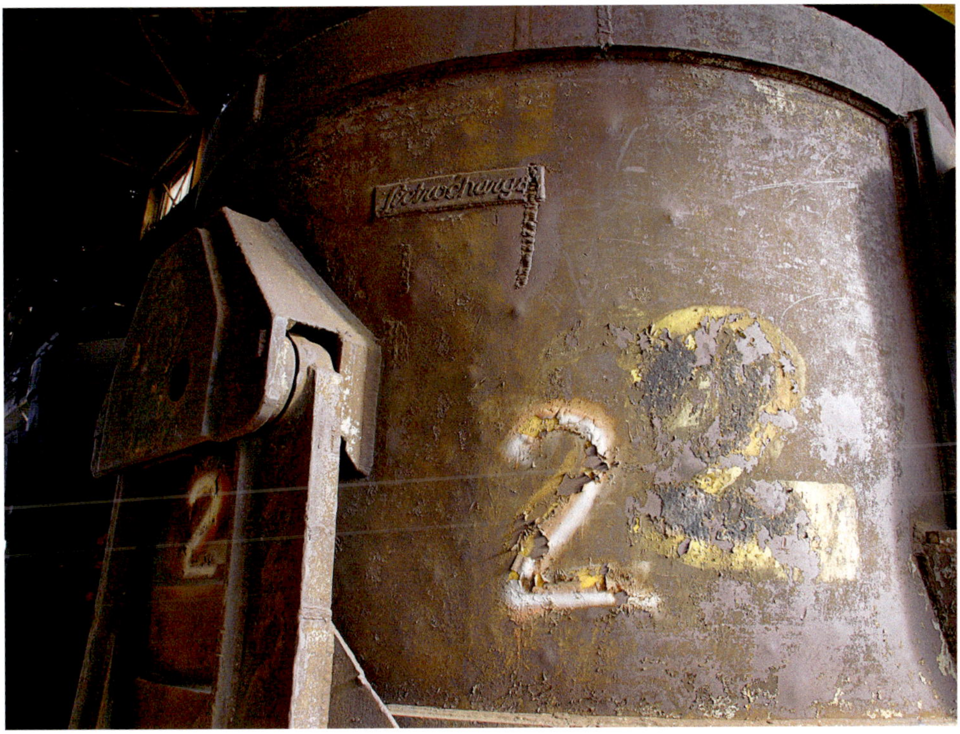

Exterior of a ladle, used in the EAF method.

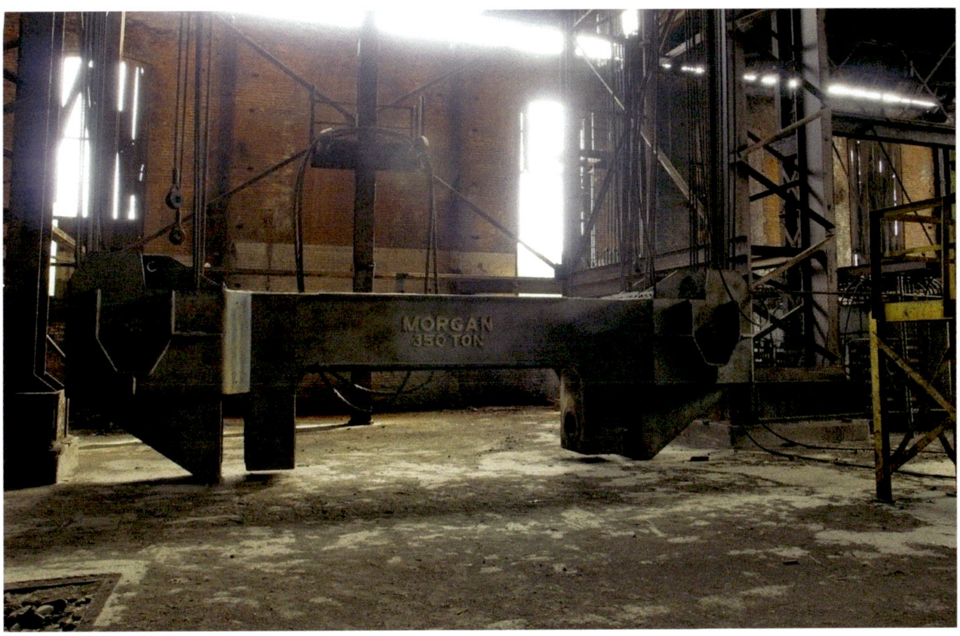

A hoist formerly operating in the Electric Furnace Melt Shop.

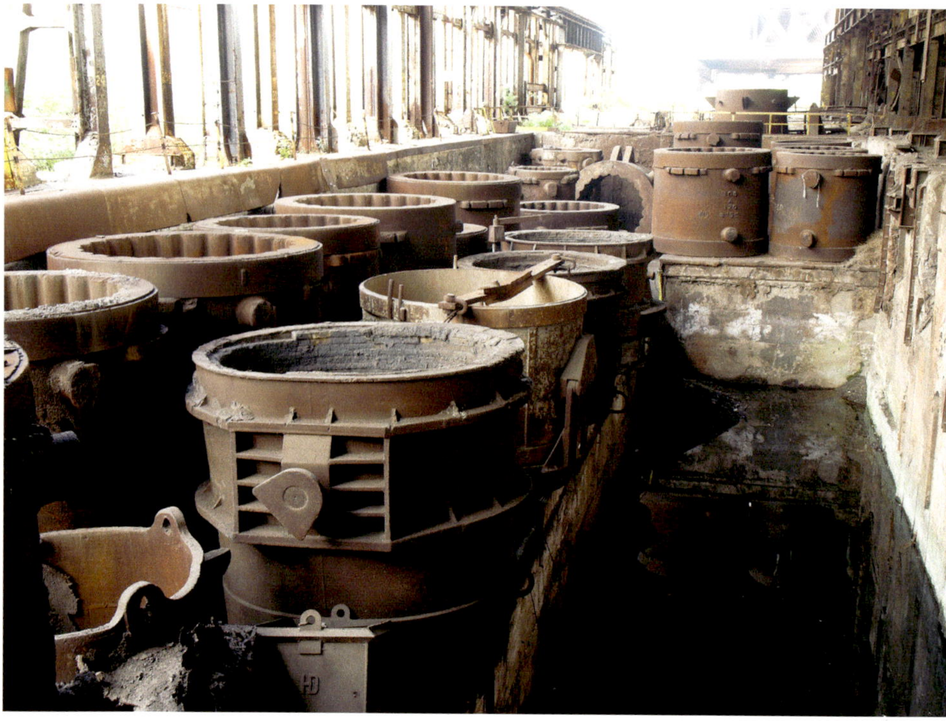

Ladles used in the Electric Furnace Melt Shop.

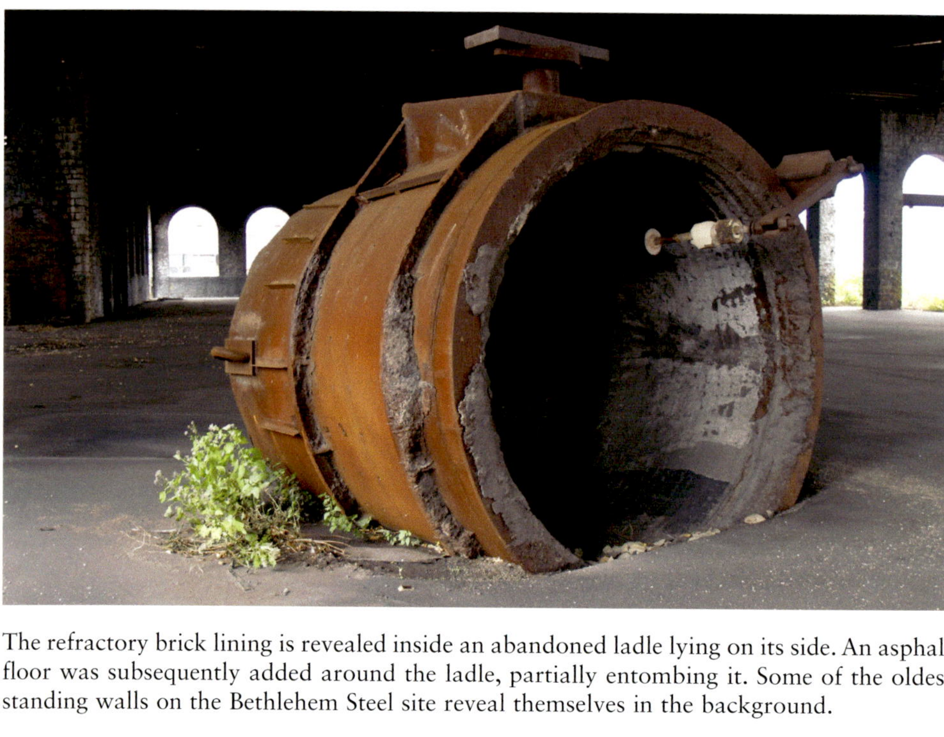

The refractory brick lining is revealed inside an abandoned ladle lying on its side. An asphalt floor was subsequently added around the ladle, partially entombing it. Some of the oldest standing walls on the Bethlehem Steel site reveal themselves in the background.

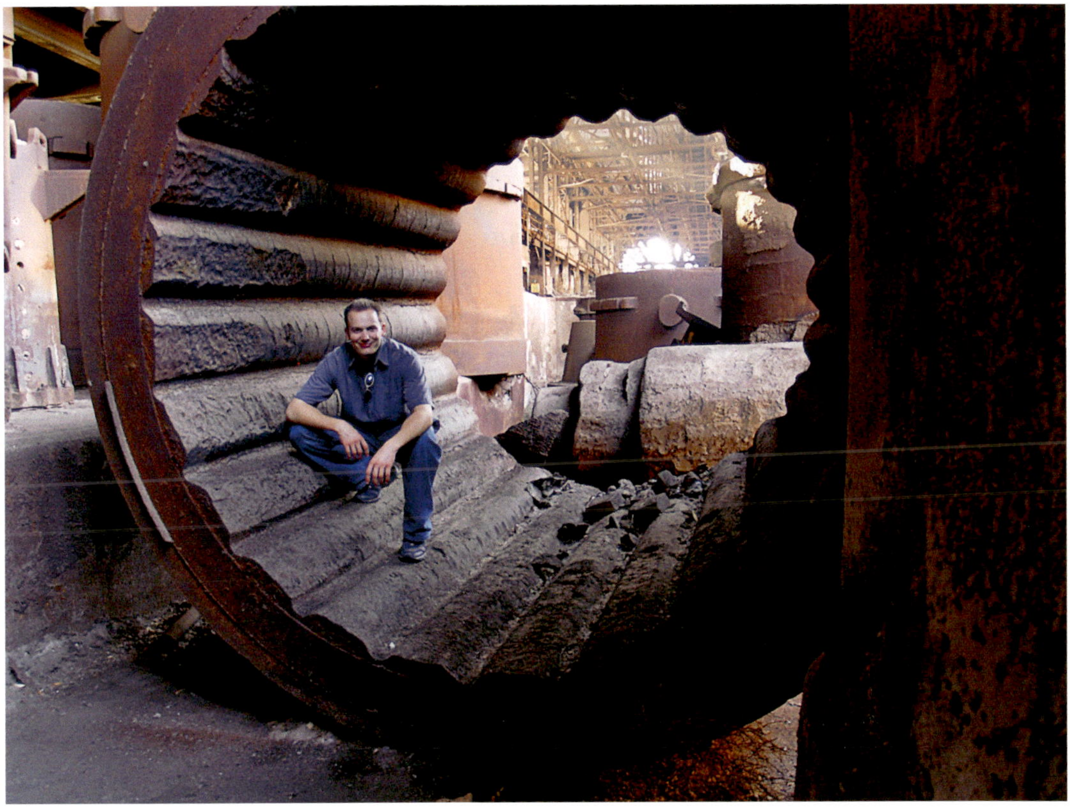

The photographer in 2006.

between corporate greed and the people, with public opinion coming down on the side of the popular president.

As the company declined, Bethlehem Steel's mining operations, raw material processing, transportation entities, and other ancillary enterprises in addition to actual steelmaking, burdened the company with high overhead costs, while no longer producing the revenue they once could. Bethlehem Steel was in desperate need to raise cash, so they started selling off some of these encumbrances to give a short-term boost to the ledgers.

On Saturday, November 18, 1995, Bethlehem Steel ceased its "hot end" operations as Blast Furnace C smelted taconite for the last time. Called "the last heat," it was an emotional time for workers who had given so much of their lives to the company. For the first time in nearly a century and a half, iron and steel were no longer being made in Bethlehem, Pennsylvania.

With the blast furnaces cold and no new steel being made from pig iron, only a limited amount of revenue was raised from selling coke to other steelmakers. Manufacturing almost nothing and divesting itself of even more assets, the company was clearly on life support.

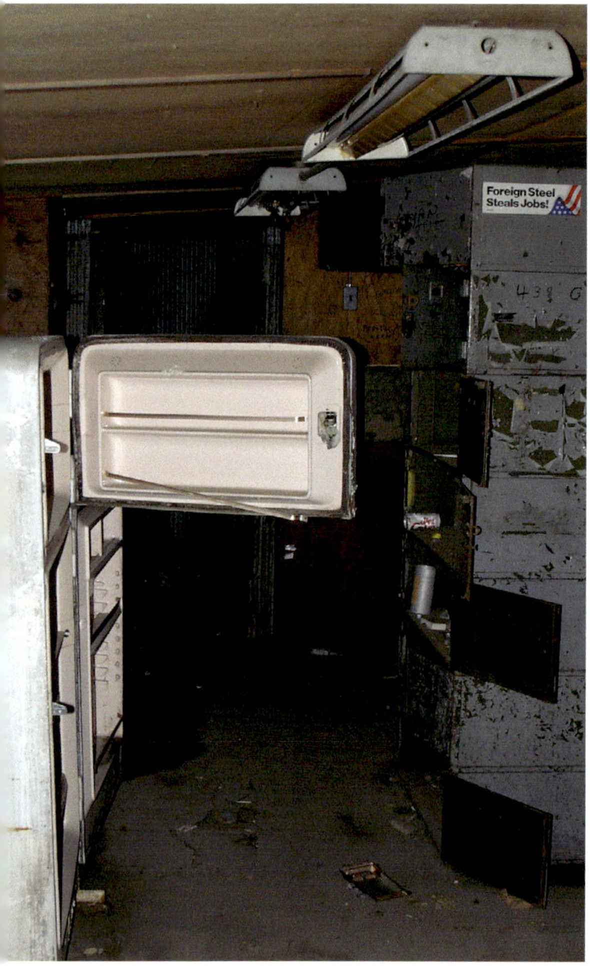

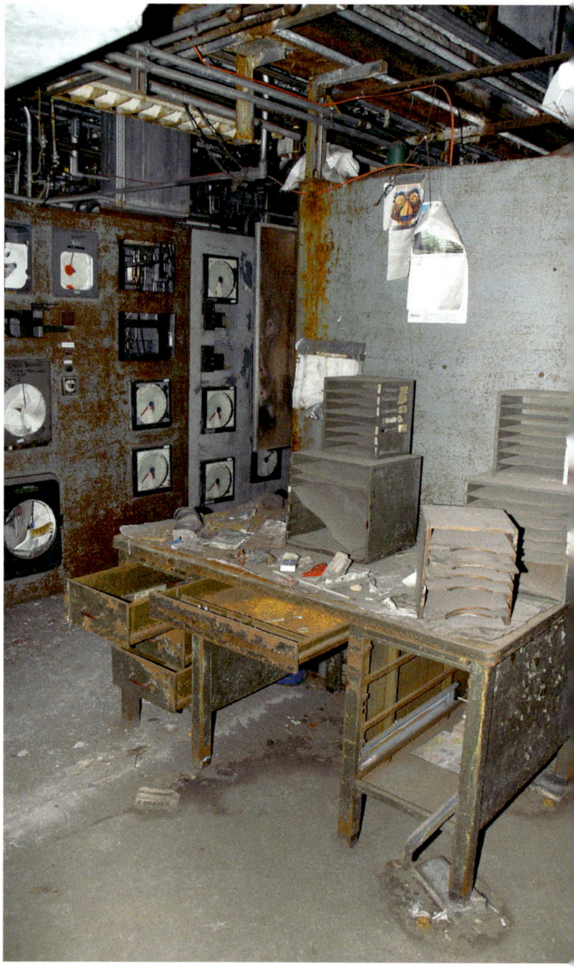

Above left: A break room with a "bumper sticker" reading "Foreign Steel Steals Jobs!"

Above right: These assorted gauges were used for monitoring stoves and the hot blast temperature entering a blast furnace. Below the open desk drawers, the paper on the floor curiously has a headline of "A PRAYER" and the subheading begins with "War," but it cannot be interpreted further.

Opposite page: This curled calendar pays tribute to the final blast furnace operation in November 1995.

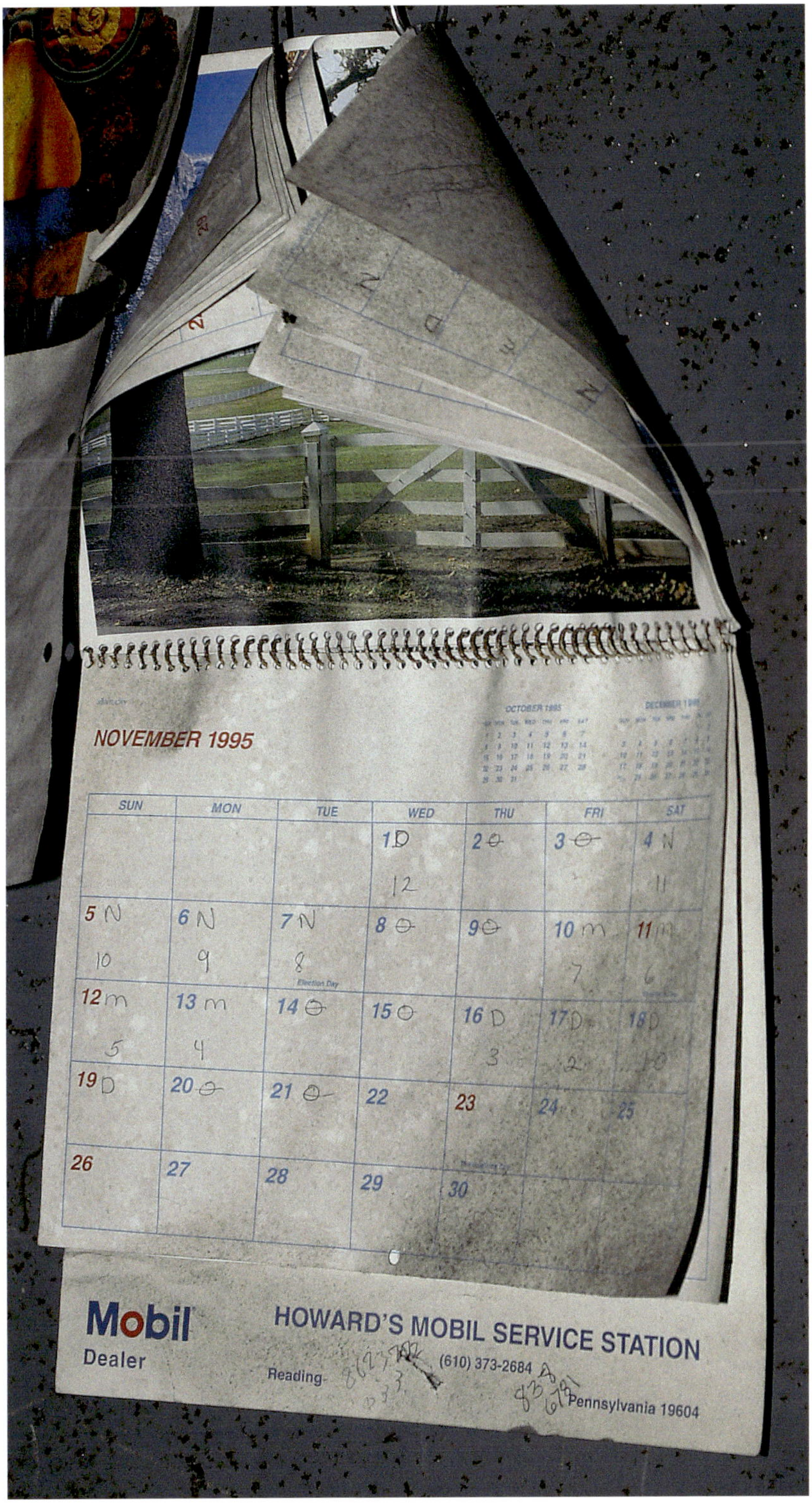
NOVEMBER 1995
SUN
MON
TUE
WED
THU
FRI
SAT
Mobil
Dealer
HOWARD'S MOBIL SERVICE STATION
Reading
(610) 373-2684
Pennsylvania 19604

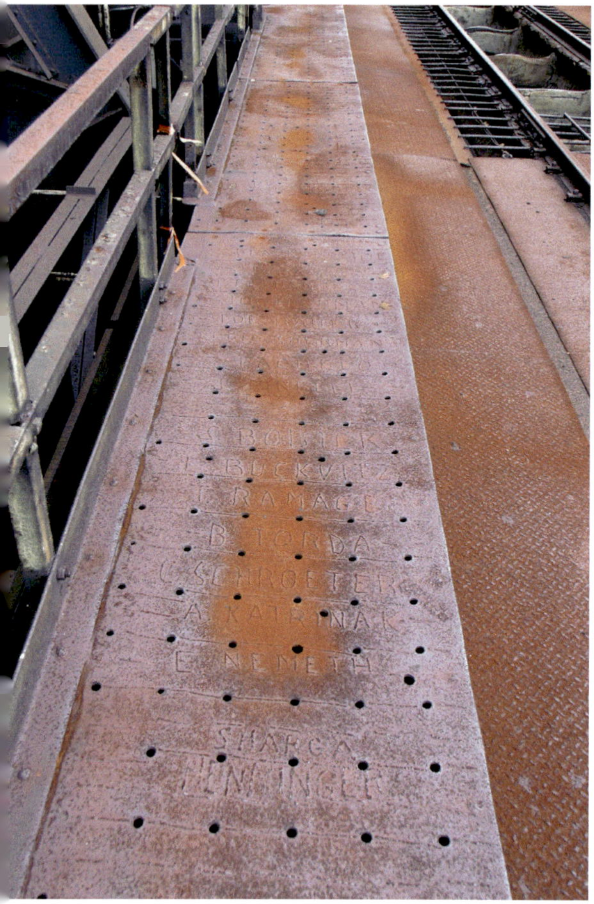

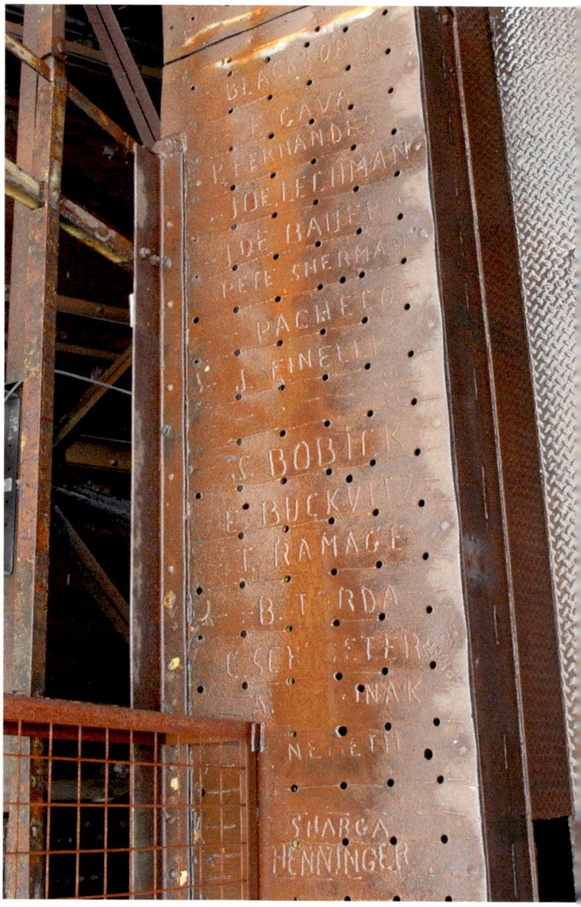

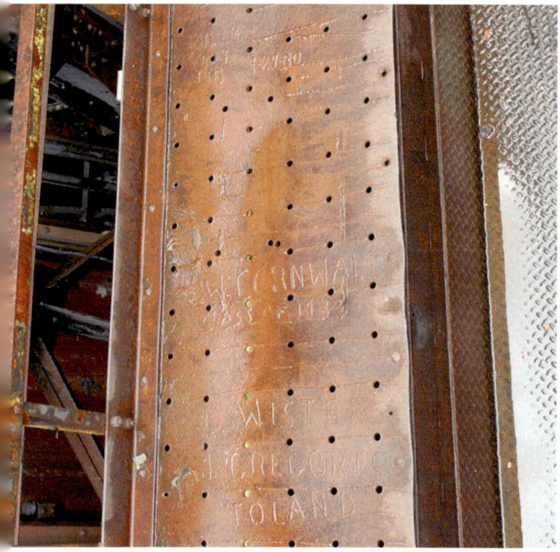

Above: Bethlehem Steel workers' names are immortalized on the railroad trestle in front of Blast Furnace D. Originally photographed in 2006; re-photographed in 2023 after rainfall for increased readability.

Left: The date "9-29-1980" in addition to "Class of 1937" accompanies the worker names on this section of trestle. Photograph taken in 2023.

Yet, it was actually Bethlehem Steel's pension system that was becoming the most dominant and onerous of all the company's problems. If a facility was closed to avoid paying workers' wages, it appeared to conserve cash, but that only accelerated the pension and retirement benefits promised to its workers.

In 1957, Bethlehem Steel had balanced its pension fund with 167,000 active workers, but toward the end of the last century, there were only 11,500 employees nationwide and 120,000 on pensions and benefits, a totally upside-down system. At the beginning of the 2000s, when The Steel was virtually bankrupt, pension payments could not be met, and the Pension Benefit Guaranty Corporation, an underwriting organization that uses no taxpayer dollars, had to step in. Although this program bailed out Bethlehem Steel pensions, medical insurance and other promised benefits were not paid, leaving some retirees with resentment toward the company.

In 2001, with more debt than assets, Bethlehem Steel filed for bankruptcy under Chapter 11. Although their stock had nearly doubled in value in 1993 with the announcement of cost reduction plans, it now plunged to under one dollar per share, and ultimately went to zero. Remaining assets were sold to International Steel Group in 2003. There was no longer an entity called Bethlehem Steel.

When "The Steel" left Bethlehem, it was devastating. However, effective, optimistic planning—plus a 2007 purchase of 126 acres of Bethlehem Steel property by Las Vegas Sands Corporation—uplifted the city. In 2019, the site with its casino, hotel, restaurants, and shops was sold to Wind Creek Hospitality, an entertainment gaming company owned by the Poarch Band of Creek Indians. Today, Bethlehem's Southside has art studios and galleries, restaurants, shops, a charter arts school, an ice rink, a PBS affiliate, ArtsQuest Center with its movie theater, indoor and outdoor entertainment venues, and café, plus the blast furnaces and remaining Bethlehem Steel buildings.

Although pig iron and virgin steel are no longer made in Bethlehem, a remnant here of "The Steel" continues operation as Lehigh Heavy Forge, a specialized steel products manufacturer and former subsidiary of Bethlehem Steel.

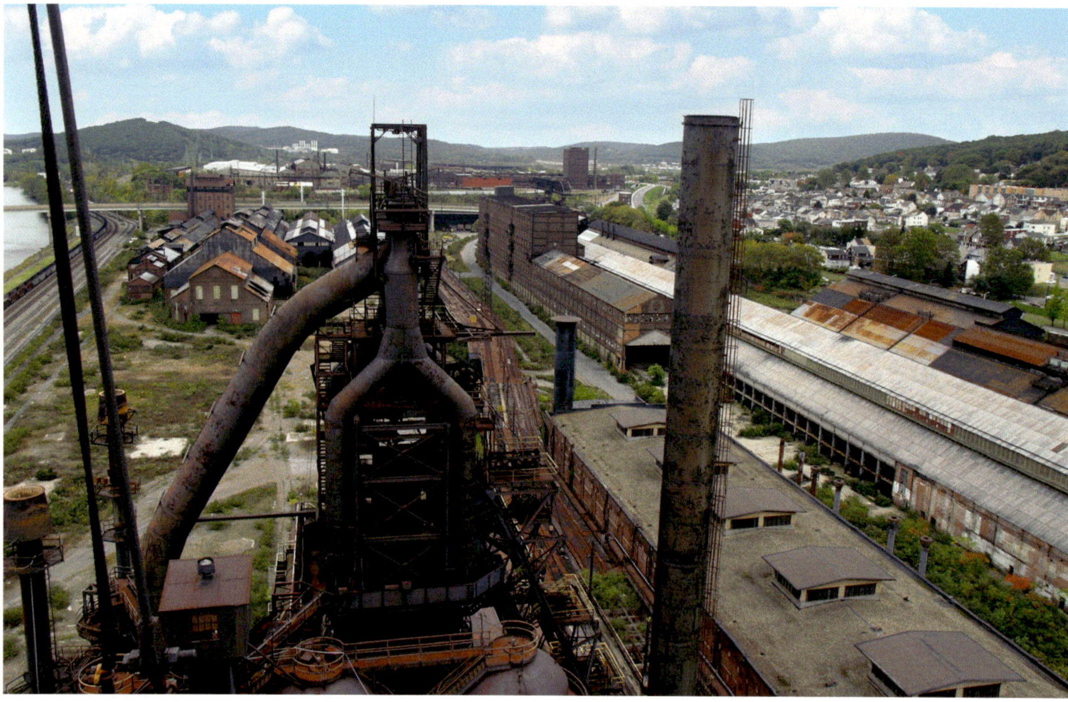

Above, below, and opposite page: Panoramic view of Southside Bethlehem from the top of Blast Furnace D.

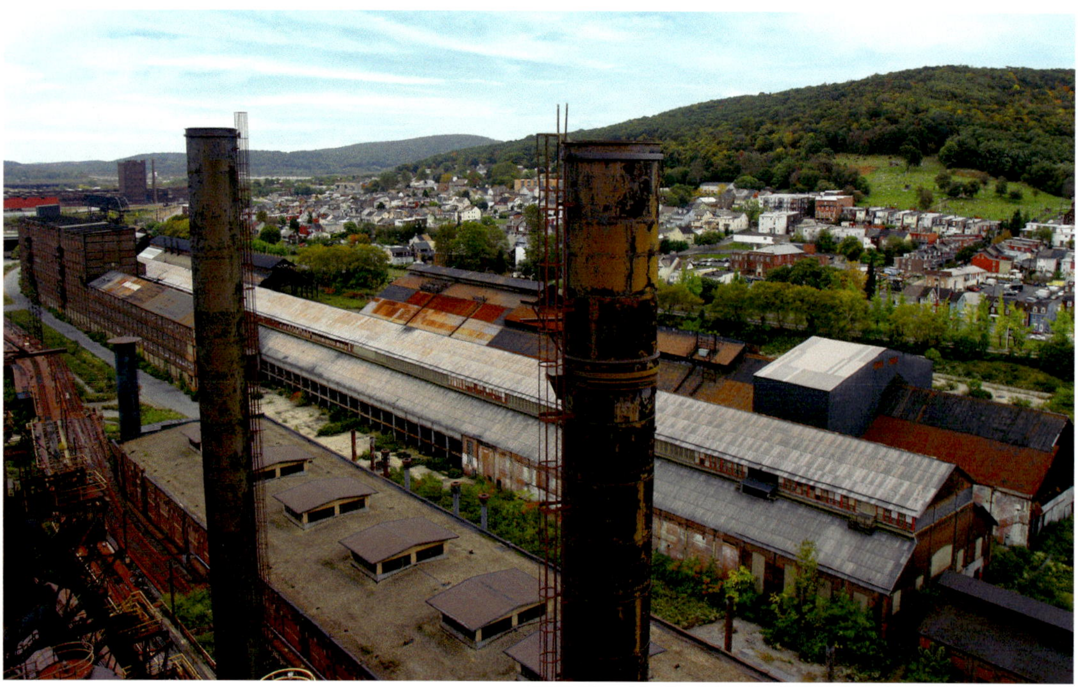

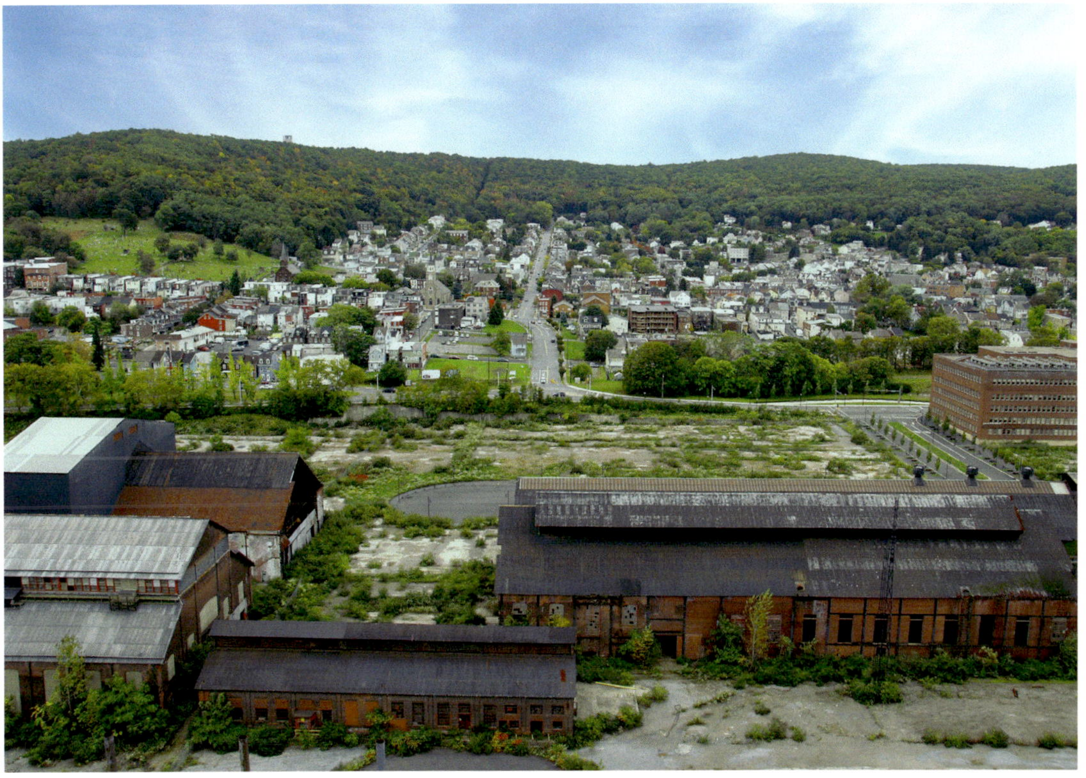

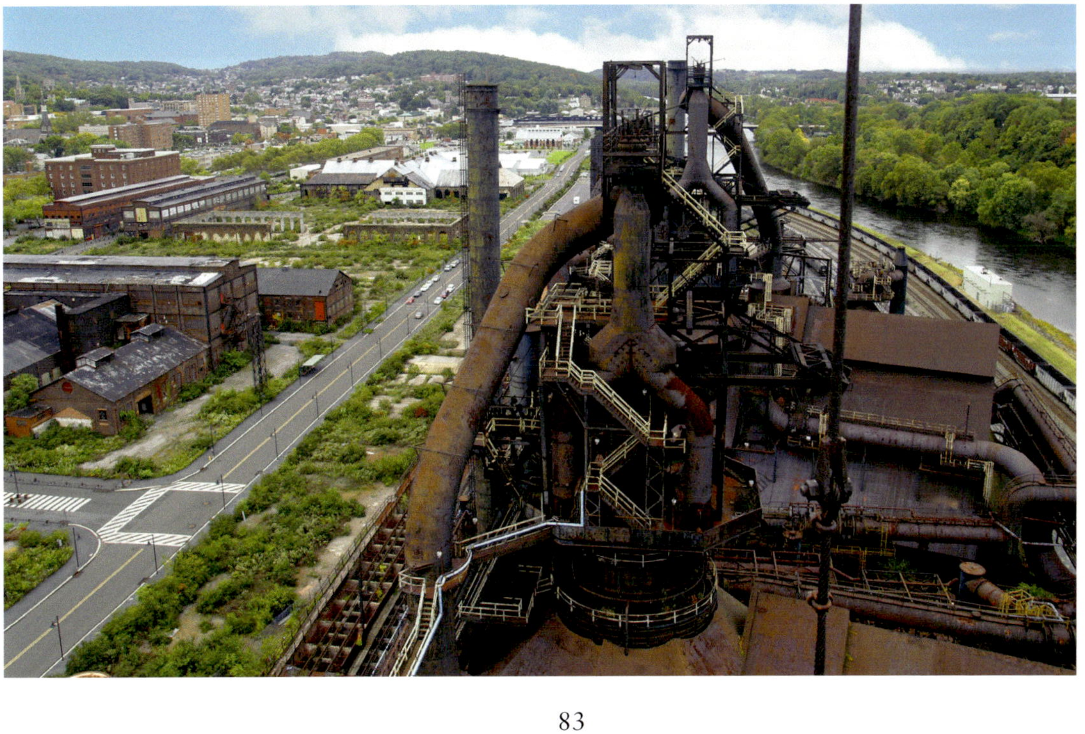

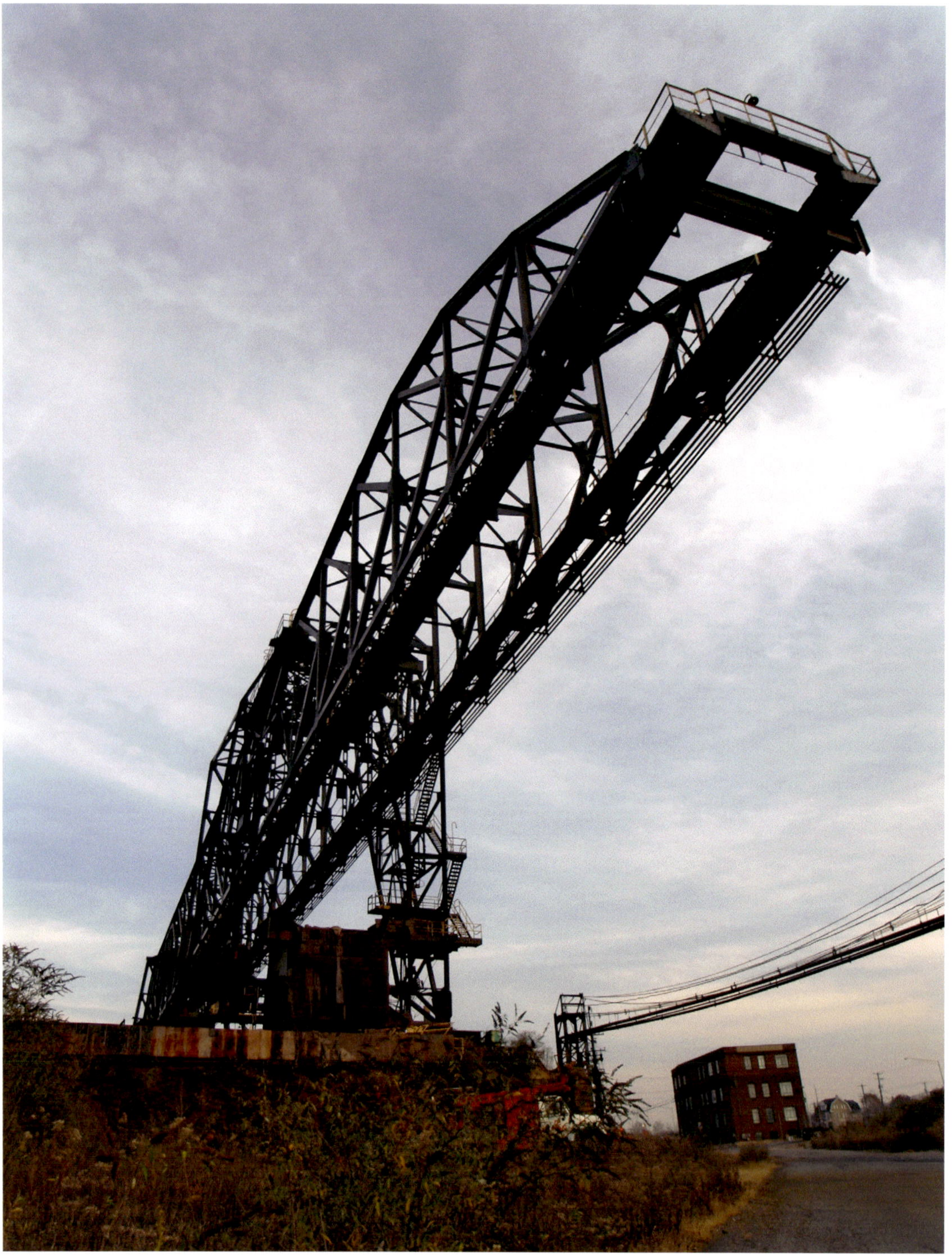

This single ore bridge (there were previously three of them) now serves as the impressive outdoor entrance to the new casino.

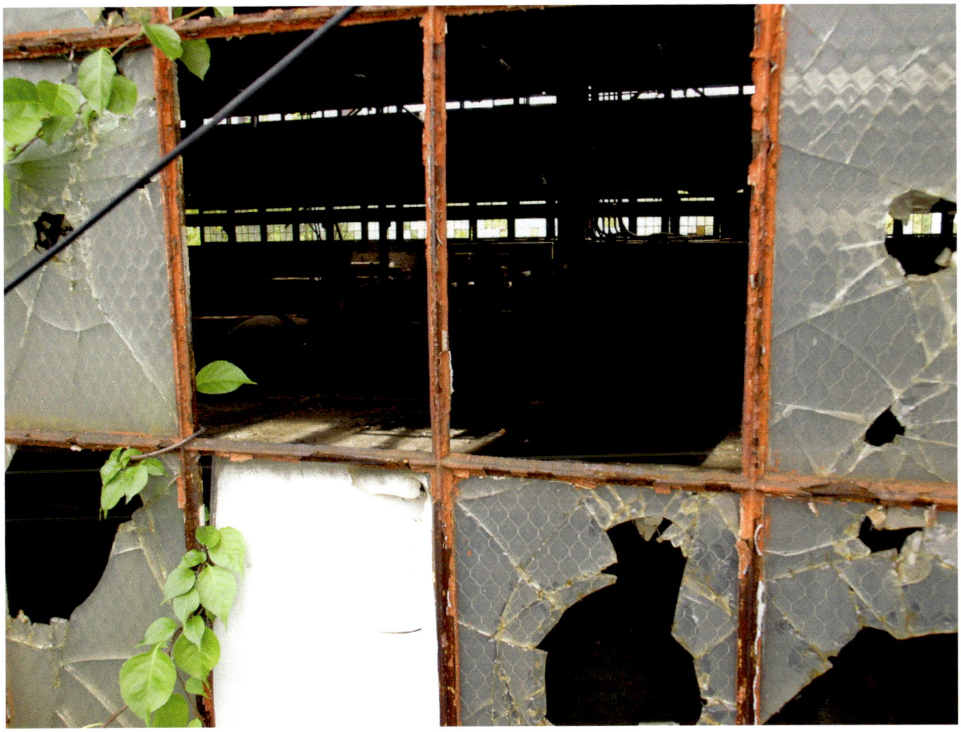

Shattered windows ... and dreams ... at Bethlehem Steel.

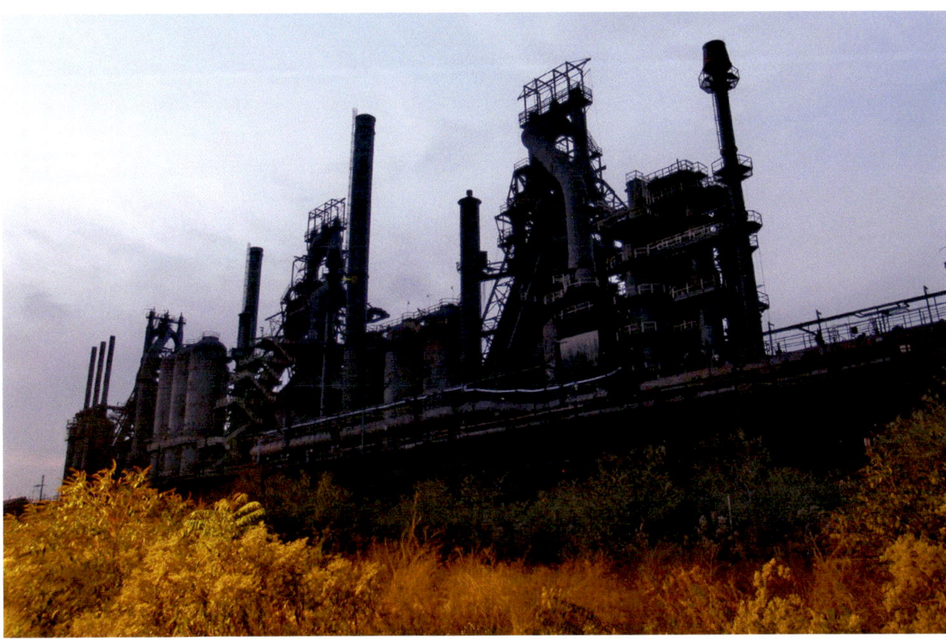

Silenced Blast Furnaces A, B, and C at sunset.

13

BUILDING AMERICA ... AND BEYOND

Although permanently gone from the corporate landscape, Bethlehem Steel has left its legacy in a myriad of buildings, bridges, and ships; tens of thousands of miles of railroad rail; countless automobiles and consumer goods ... in everything from warships to home refrigerators. Of course, some products are in junkyards or have been recycled, but others still proudly stand, like New York's George Washington Bridge, Chicago's Merchandise Mart, and Washington DC's Supreme Court Building. All across the country, Bethlehem Steel has helped build America.

Some structures made of Bethlehem Steel have become icons of a city, like San Francisco's Golden Gate Bridge and Alcatraz. The University of Pittsburgh's most prominent building, the Cathedral of Learning, is actually built of Bethlehem Steel, despite being in the very heart of competitor United States Steel's corporate headquarters. Philadelphia's Commodore Barry and Ben Franklin bridges; Virginia's Chesapeake Bay Bridge; the Peace Bridge between Buffalo, New York, and Fort Erie, Ontario; and Maine/New Hampshire's Piscataqua River Bridge, among many others, were all built with Bethlehem Steel.

In New York City, Rockefeller Plaza, Lincoln Center, Madison Square Garden, the Waldorf Astoria, the Lincoln Tunnel, the Empire State Building, and the Verrazano Narrows Bridge all contain varying percentages of Bethlehem Steel. In fact, in the 1940s, nearly 80 percent of the New York skyline was built with steel that Bethlehem made.

Steel products from Bethlehem have been in as diverse items from the past as the axle of the Ferris Wheel at the Chicago World's Columbian Exposition (1893), the engine cylinders of Charles Lindbergh's *Spirit of St. Louis* airplane (1927), multiple-unit railroad passenger cars for use in southeastern Pennsylvania (1931), and piping as well as the structure supporting the concrete of Hoover Dam (1936).

Early ships and armament built by The Steel's shipbuilding divisions began a distinguished lineage. In 1882, the United States government saw the need to modernize the Navy, and to do it with steel. Bethlehem built the USS *Texas*, an early battleship commissioned just before World War I. Dubbed "the arsenal of democracy," Bethlehem Steel produced 60 percent of the guns and 45 percent of the artillery shells ordered by the government during the "Great War."

Even more significant was the role Bethlehem Steel played in helping win World War II. President Franklin D. Roosevelt, recognizing the number of ships lost early in the United States involvement in the war, asked Bethlehem Steel to produce "a ship a day" for the Allied war effort. Expanding its existing shipbuilding division, The Steel answered the call, building 1,121 ships of all sorts, from battleships to Liberty Ships, including the structure as well as gun barrels, turrets, and other armament. Fearing sabotage to war production, Bethlehem employed female security guards, arming them with .38-caliber revolvers. They became known as "Pistol Packin' Mamas."

Number 2 Machine Shop, a very long building still standing on the Bethlehem property, built components of the ships and sent them by rail to port facilities at Brooklyn Navy Yard, New York; Sparrows Point, Maryland; and other locations for assembly and launching. Among ships built was the USS *Missouri*, upon which the Japanese surrendered to end the war and presently a floating memorial at Pearl Harbor, Hawaii.

After the war, Bethlehem Steel built many long, high-capacity ships. The Great Lakes Steamship Division built the first 1,000-foot-long ship for Great Lakes service. The *Stewart J. Cort* was launched in 1972 and represented the first of a dozen exceptionally long freighters.

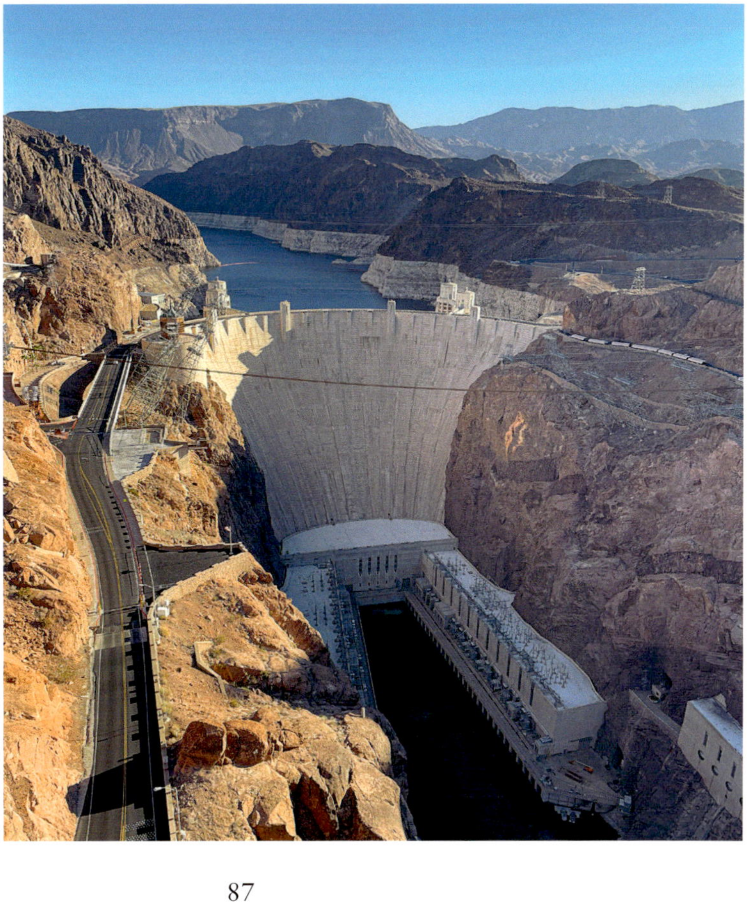

Hoover Dam on the Colorado River. Photograph taken in 2023.

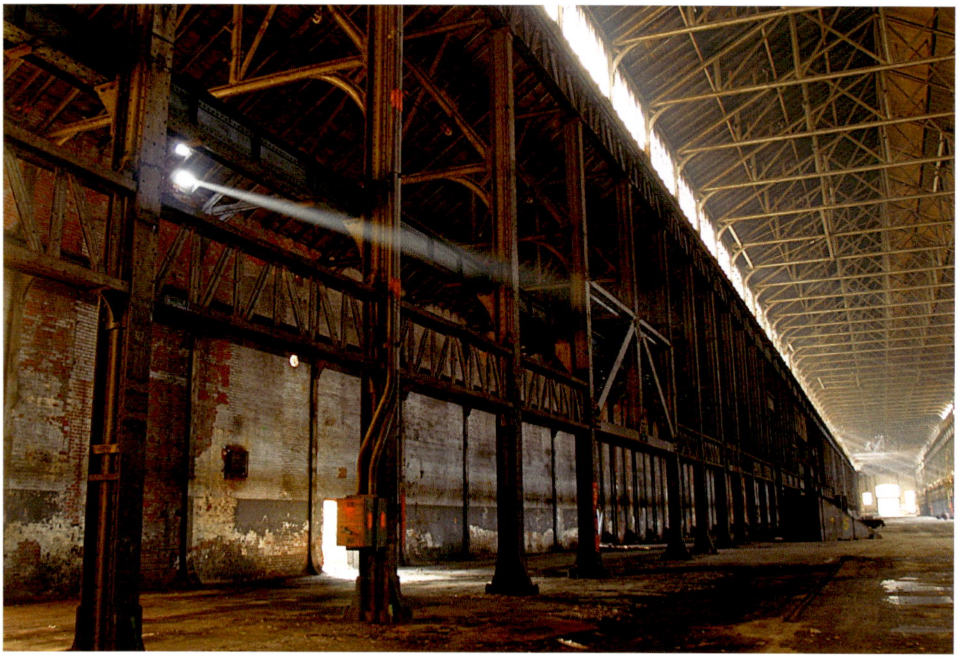

The Number 2 Machine Shop, which upon completion set a record for building length, is approximately ⅓-mile-long from end to end.

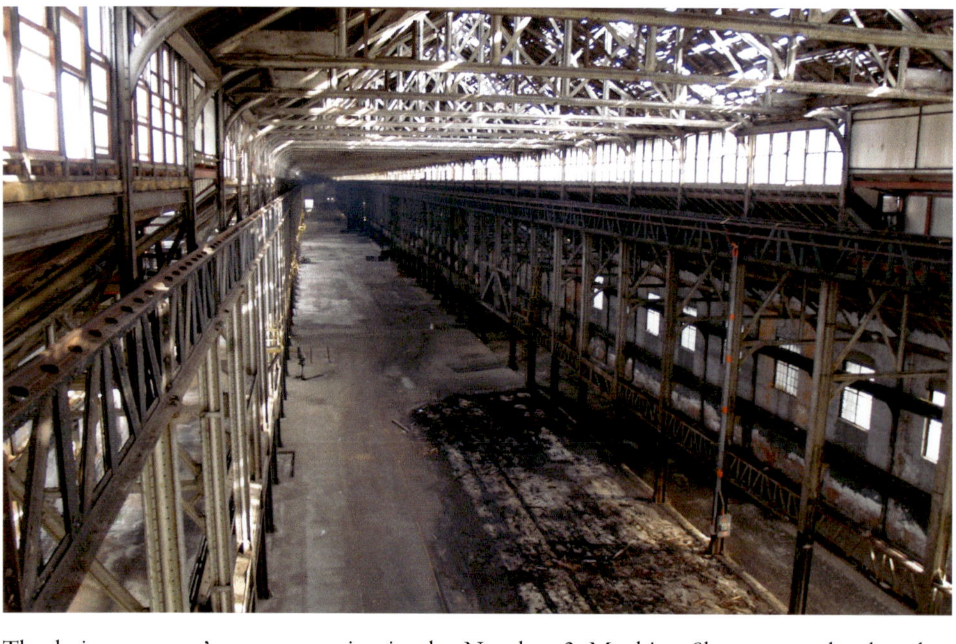

The hoist operator's vantage point in the Number 2 Machine Shop, now desolate but formerly bustling with hundreds of machinists and diverse projects.

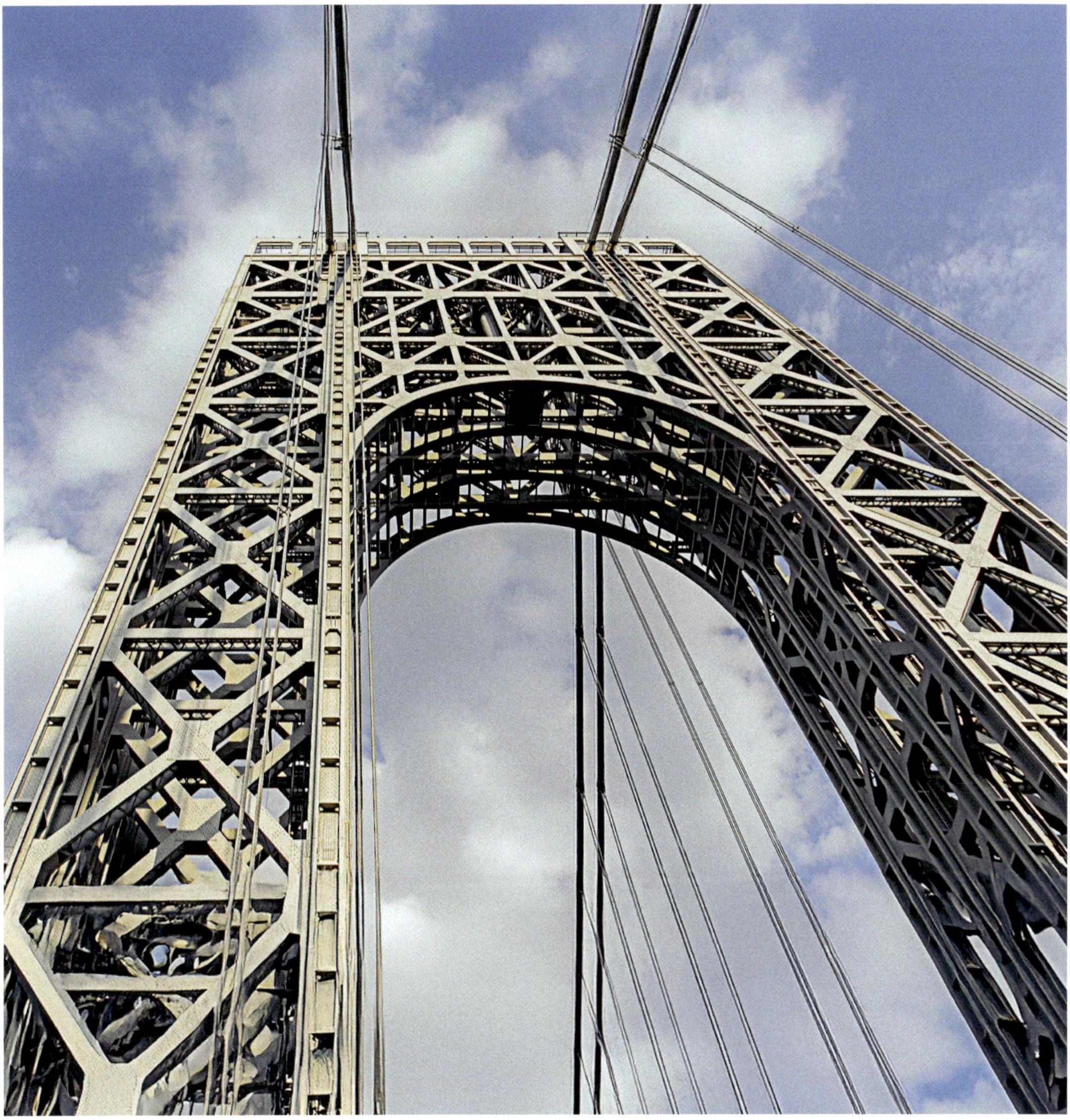

One of the George Washington Bridge towers, New York. The original design called for the tower structures to be encased in concrete and granite, but the Great Depression financial situation prevented this. (*photograph credit: Bigstock.com*)

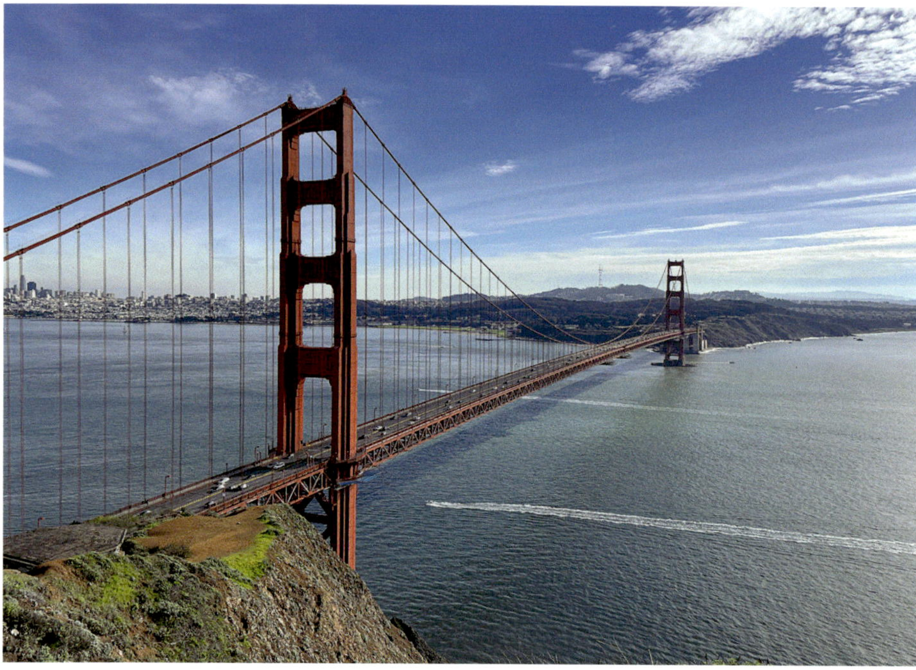

The Golden Gate Bridge "international orange" paint strikes a stunning contrast against the sea and sky in California. Photograph taken in 2024.

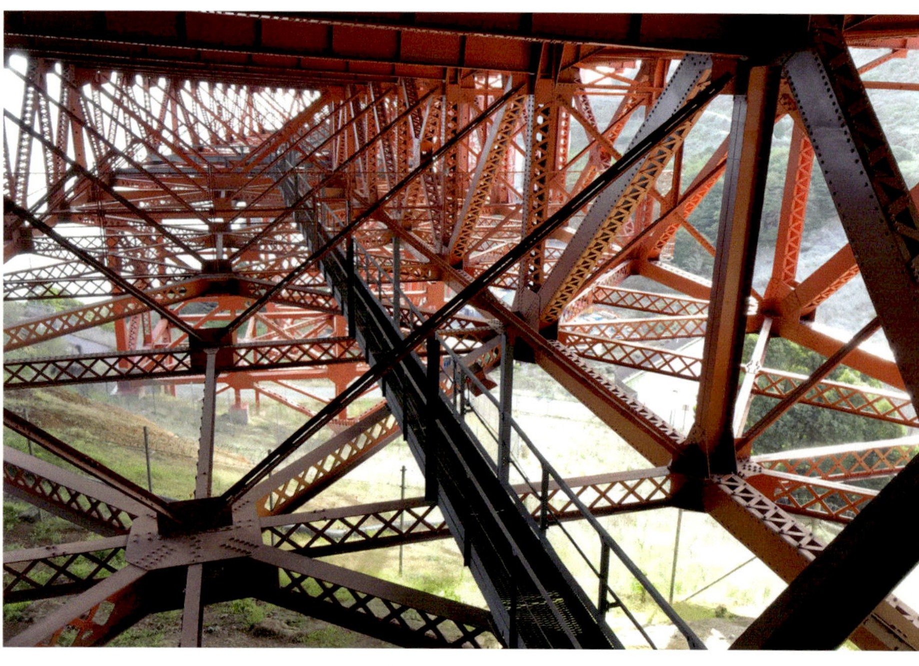

A beautiful maze of riveted steel lattice forms the deck truss underneath the Golden Gate Bridge roadway. Photograph taken in 2018.

14

EPILOGUE

Bethlehem Steel was a positive and progressive influence on America, connecting people with bridges and railroad rail; advancing culture, commerce, and education with buildings; helping to win two world wars; providing products for transportation and industry; and supplying the material for countless consumer goods for generations. Bethlehem Steel is gone, but America is glad that it happened.

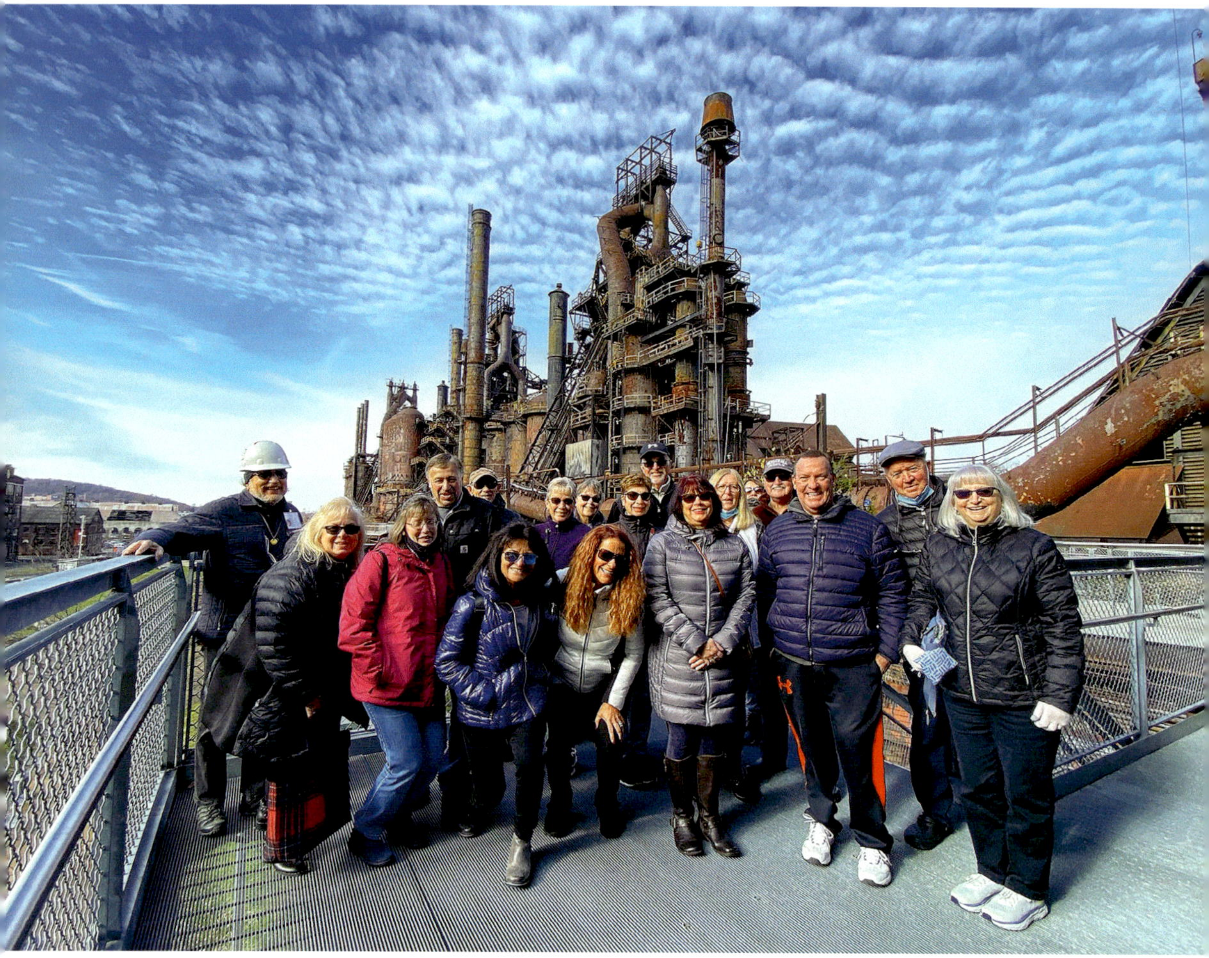

A tour group that John K. Landis hosted in 2021. He appears on the left wearing a white hard hat.

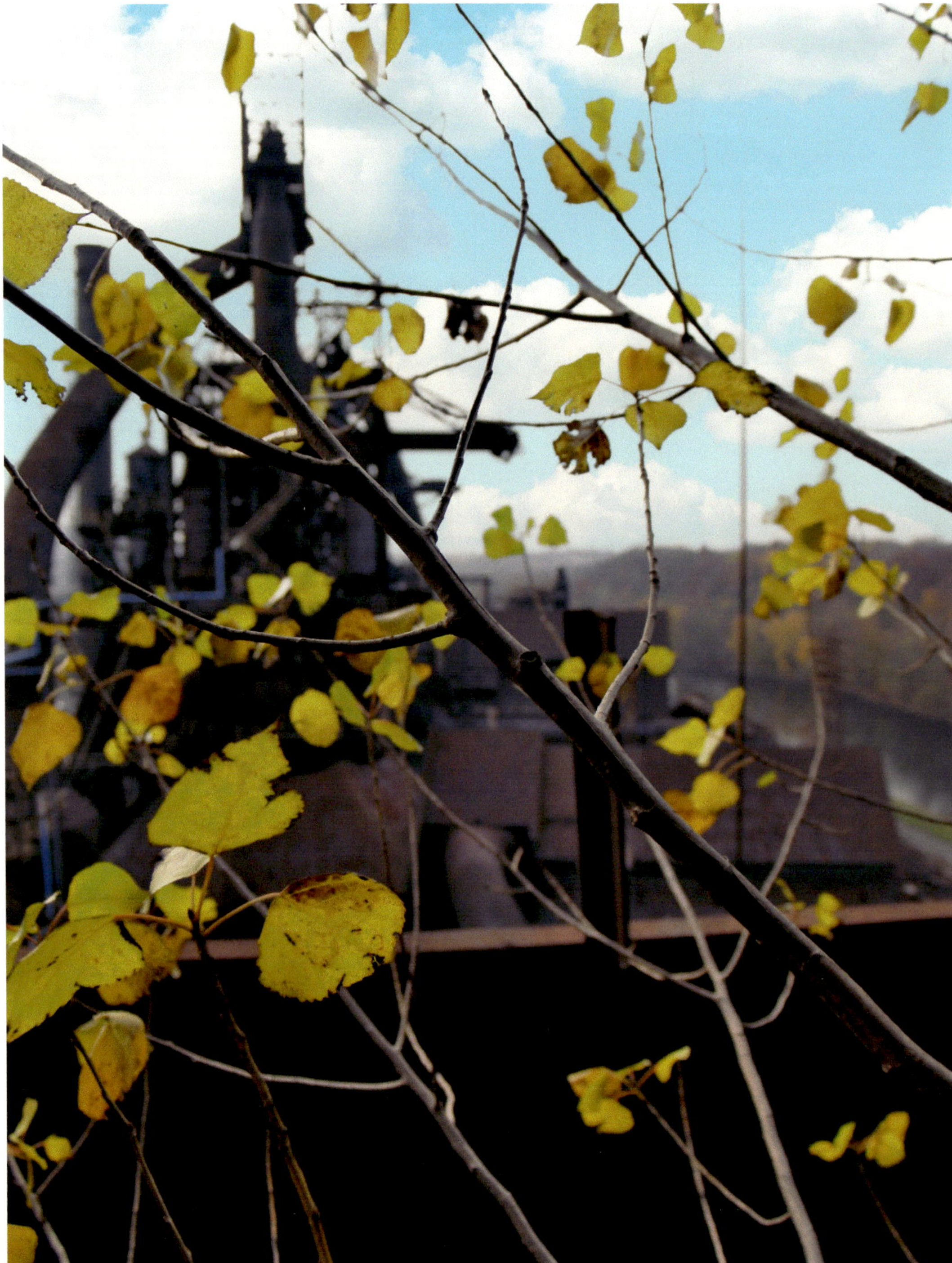

The autumn leaf color of a sapling that took root in the ore and ash debris partway up Blast Furnace D. Blast Furnace C appears in the background.

BIBLIOGRAPHY

Blalock, T., "First-Hand: Tales from The Steel," *Engineering and Technological History Wiki (ETHW)*, March 16, 2015.

Garn, A., *Bethlehem Steel* (Princeton, NJ: Princeton Architectural Press, 2000).

Heiliczer, J., "The Dorr Plant at Bethlehem Steel," brokenbushandroundtop.com, accessed March 23, 2023.

Henkin, A., "Women of Steel" [Radio broadcast], WYPR Baltimore, wypr.com (February 17, 2021).

"Introduction to Continuous Casting." Continuous Casting Consortium, ccc.illinois.edu/introduction/intro.html, accessed March 22, 2023.

Jurgen, K. H., "Steel Plants: Size, Location, and Design," *Encyclopedia of Materials: Science and Technology*, pp. 8,824–8,832. (Amsterdam: Elsevier Books & Journals), accessed March 21, 2023.

Kennedy, J., "US1630088A - Elevator tower for blast-furnace structures," patents.google.com. patents.google.com > patent (accessed July 23, 2023).

Loomis, C. J., "The Sinking of Bethlehem Steel," *Fortune*, Vol. 149, No. 7, pp. 174–187 (New York: Fortune Media Group Holdings, 2004).

"Mike Korb Mining Collection." *Bethlehem Mines Corporation, National Museum of American History*, ial.lyrasistechnology.org/repositories, accessed March 6, 2023.

Piersa, M., "Virtual Museum: Blowing Engines" [YouTube], *National Museum of Industrial History*, nmih.org (May 13, 2020).

"Principles of Extractive Metallurgy," *Metallurgy of Iron and Steel*, chem.libretexts.org, August 25, 2020.

Reutter, M., *Making Steel: Sparrows Point and the Rise and Ruin of American Industrial Might* (New York: Summit Books, 1988).

Yeakel, N. S., *Bethlehem Steel Railroading* (Hanover, PA: The Railroad Press, 2008).

The National Museum of Industrial History was useful in information verification on certain topics. The photographs of raw materials, molten/hot metal, steel beams, and George Washington Bridge were purchased from Bigstock.com. The photograph of hot metal bottle cars was downloaded from FreeImages.com.

ABOUT THE PHOTOGRAPHER AND AUTHORS

Steven M. Landis works as a key account manager in the automotive industry, where he has been employed in a variety of roles for two decades. He is an inventor and creative writer, enjoys the agony and elation of mountain climbing, and loves photographing the beautiful, bizarre, and especially hard-to-access or abandoned places. He regrets having been too young to ever have worked at Bethlehem Steel but counts the rare access he had exploring and photographing the hallowed grounds of the former flagship plant—where so much of modern U.S. and global history was written—as being among the best moments in his life.

John K. Landis, a steel plant tour guide with Historic Bethlehem Museums and Sites, is often asked if he worked for Bethlehem Steel. He is in fact a graphic designer and professor emeritus of art. But, on tour days, he feels like he does work for this icon of American heavy industry, albeit as a "looper," the name Bethlehem Steel gave to management trainees on a "loop course" around the plant as they learned about the company. It is with this perspective that John wrote text to accompany the photographs, awed as he is by the beauty of our industrial heritage and eager to pass along his continuously evolving knowledge of the might and majesty of the steel industry of the past.

Steven and John may be contacted at: urban.exploration.photographer@gmail.com.

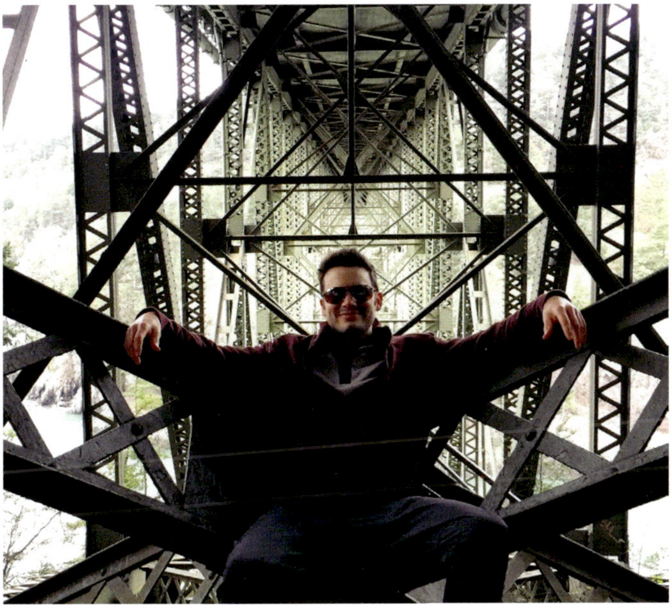

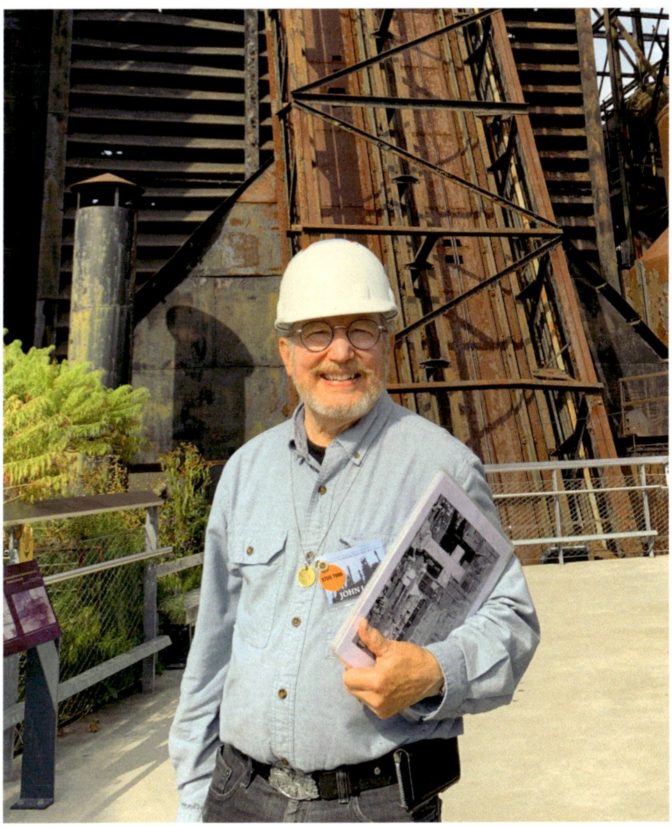